French
Essentials
FOR
DUMMIES

by Laura K. Lawless and
Zoe Erotopoulos, PhD

WILEY

Wiley Publishing, Inc.

French Essentials For Dummies®

Published by
Wiley Publishing, Inc.
111 River St.
Hoboken, NJ 07030-5774

www.wiley.com

WILEY

About the Authors

Laura K. Lawless is the author of seven language instruction books (four French and three Spanish). She also teaches French, Spanish, and English on the Internet and has a Web site of vegetarian recipes and information.

Zoe Erotopoulos holds an M.A., M.Phil, and Ph.D. in French and Romance Philology from Columbia University. Her French teaching experience ranges from elementary to advance level courses including literature and theater. Dr. Erotopoulos has taught at a number of institutions including Columbia University, Reid Hall in Paris, and Trinity College in Hartford, Connecticut. For the past 15 years, she has been teaching in the Department of Modern Languages and Literatures at Fairfield University in Fairfield, Connecticut.

Publisher's Acknowledgments

We're proud of this book; please send us your comments at http://dummies.custhelp.com. For other comments, please contact our Customer Care Department within the U.S. at 877-762-2974, outside the U.S. at 317-572-3993, or fax 317-572-4002.

Some of the people who helped bring this book to market include the following:

Acquisitions, Editorial, and Media Development

Project Editor: Joan Friedman

Acquisitions Editor: Michael Lewis

Assistant Editor: David Lutton

Technical Editors: Hoi Ngoc Doan, Eric Laird, Beverly Randall

Senior Editorial Manager: Jennifer Ehrlich

Editorial Supervisor and Reprint Editor: Carmen Krikorian

Editorial Assistant: Rachelle S. Amick

Cover Photos: © iStockphoto.com / Ivonne Wierink-vanWetten

Cartoon: Rich Tennant (www.the5thwave.com)

Composition Services

Project Coordinator: Kristie Rees

Layout and Graphics: Claudia Bell, Samantha K. Cherolis, Corrie Socolovitch

Proofreader: Mildred Rosenzweig

Indexer: Estalita Slivoskey

Publishing and Editorial for Consumer Dummies

   Diane Graves Steele, Vice President and Publisher, Consumer Dummies

   Kristin Ferguson-Wagstaffe, Product Development Director, Consumer Dummies

   Ensley Eikenburg, Associate Publisher, Travel

   Kelly Regan, Editorial Director, Travel

Publishing for Technology Dummies

   Andy Cummings, Vice President and Publisher, Dummies Technology/General User

Composition Services

   Debbie Stailey, Director of Composition Services

Contents at a Glance

Table of Contents

Introduction

*W*hether you're taking a French class in high school or college, this handy reference book can help you recall vocabulary, verb conjugation, crucial differences between French and English, and much more. If the idea of snuggling up with your textbook in advance of a big exam makes you queasy, take heart: This book is a focused, straightforward review of the key material covered in introductory French courses. *French Essentials For Dummies* can help you reach your goals painlessly and effortlessly as you enhance your French language skills.

French Essentials For Dummies provides you with all the basic grammar you need to know to understand the language and to communicate it clearly. With the help of this book, you'll find it a snap to have a conversation about topics other than your name and the weather. And that's quite an achievement!

About This Book

We designed this book to be as accessible as possible. Each self-contained chapter presents a different topic that allows you to master essential French skills. We cover just the basics of each topic so you can get a quick refresher of what you've learned in your coursework. Plus, we include plenty of examples to reinforce the rules so that you're exposed to colloquial, everyday, correct French that native speakers expect to hear from someone using their language.

Conventions Used in This Book

To make this book as easy to use as possible, we use two important conventions throughout:

- ✔ French words and sentences, as well as endings we want to highlight, are set in **boldface** to make them stand out.

- ✔ English equivalents, set in *italic,* follow the French examples.

Foolish Assumptions

We wrote this book with the following assumptions in mind:

- ✔ You've taken — or are taking — an introductory French class either at the high school or college level.

- ✔ You want to review what you've already learned so you can pass a test for your course or excel on a college placement exam.

- ✔ You want a thorough book but one that isn't so advanced that you get bogged down by the rules. We try to explain French grammar as simply as possible without using too many technical terms.

- ✔ You use French at work or school and want to improve your writing or speaking skills. Maybe a family member or significant other is studying French and you want to help (even though you haven't looked at a verb conjugation for years). Or you're planning a trip to France or another French-speaking country and want to put your French into practice.

Icons Used in This Book

Like all *For Dummies* books, this one uses icons to indicate certain kinds of content. You can see them in the left-hand column throughout the book. Here's what they mean:

The Remember icon points out important concepts that you need to store in the back of your mind because you'll use them quite regularly.

We use Tip icons to give you time-saving information that makes your studies quick and effective.

This icon points out certain differences between English and French that you may find confusing. To learn how French constructions differ from those in English, consult these icons.

Where to Go from Here

French Essentials For Dummies is organized to let you read only what you want to read. Each chapter stands on its own and doesn't require that you complete any of the other chapters in the book. This setup saves you a lot of time if you've mastered certain topics but feel a bit insecure about others. Take a look at the table of contents or index, pick a topic, and go! Or you may want to proceed methodically by starting at the very beginning. It's up to you!

Go ahead! Jump right in and get your feet wet. If you don't know where to begin, take time to look at the table of contents and choose the topic that seems to best fit your abilities and needs. If you're timid because you feel that your background hasn't prepared you enough, you can start at the very beginning and work your way through the book.

No matter how you choose to read *French Essentials For Dummies*, we're confident that it can help you improve your French writing and speaking skills. Of course, you shouldn't let your practice end here. Write to a French pen pal, visit French websites and message boards, rent foreign flicks from the library, attempt conversations with your French-speaking friends, or try to translate song lyrics into French while you're stuck in traffic. And when you have a grammar question, come back here and look it up. Pretty soon, the thoughts running through your head may take on a decidedly French flair. *Bonne chance!* (Good luck!)

The 5th Wave

By Rich Tennant

"Here's something. It's a language school that will teach you to speak French for $500, or for $200 they'll just give you an accent."

Chapter 1

Getting Down to Basics

• •

In This Chapter

▶ Counting with cardinal and ordinal numbers

▶ Expressing dates

▶ Telling time

▶ Reviewing parts of speech

• •

*B*eing able to use cardinal and ordinal numbers and recognizing parts of speech are essential French skills. Knowing these basics will help you perfect your oral and written French.

Using Numbers

Numbers are one of the most basic and useful parts of language. In addition to simple counting, you need *cardinal numbers* for communicating dates, time, prices, phone numbers, addresses, and so much more. You use *ordinal numbers* to express the number of a floor or the order of a person in a race or competition.

Counting with cardinal numbers

Cardinal numbers are for counting, and the low numbers are easy. You may already know them backwards and forwards, but if not, all you need to do is memorize them. The higher numbers get a bit more complicated. Check out the following list of French numbers from 0 to 1 billion.

0 **zéro**	71 **soixante et onze**
1 **un(e)**	72 **soixante-douze**
2 **deux**	73 **soixante-treize**
3 **trois**	74 **soixante-quatorze**
4 **quatre**	75 **soixante-quinze**
5 **cinq**	76 **soixante-seize**
6 **six**	77 **soixante-dix-sept**
7 **sept**	78 **soixante-dix-huit**
8 **huit**	79 **soixante-dix-neuf**
9 **neuf**	80 **quatre-vingts**
10 **dix**	81 **quatre-vingt-un**
11 **onze**	89 **quatre-vingt-neuf**
12 **douze**	90 **quatre-vingt-dix**
13 **treize**	91 **quatre-vingt-onze**
14 **quatorze**	92 **quatre-vingt-douze**
15 **quinze**	93 **quatre-vingt-treize**
16 **seize**	94 **quatre-vingt-quatorze**
17 **dix-sept**	95 **quatre-vingt-quinze**
18 **dix-huit**	96 **quatre-vingt-seize**
19 **dix-neuf**	97 **quatre-vingt-dix-sept**
20 **vingt**	98 **quatre-vingt-dix-huit**
21 **vingt et un**	99 **quatre-vingt-dix-neuf**
22 **vingt-deux**	100 **cent**
30 **trente**	101 **cent un**
31 **trente et un**	200 **deux cents**
33 **trente-trois**	201 **deux cent un**
40 **quarante**	320 **trois cent vingt**
41 **quarante et un**	1,000 **mille**
45 **quarante-cinq**	1,001 **mille un**
70 **soixante-dix**	

50 **cinquante**	1,100 **mille cent/onze cents**
51 **cinquante et un**	2,000 **deux mille**
56 **cinquante-six**	100,000 **cent mille**
60 **soixante**	1,000,000 **un million**
61 **soixante et un**	2,000,000 **deux millions**
68 **soixante-huit**	1 billion **un milliard**

Note the following about cardinal numbers:

✔ The conjunction **et** (*and*) is used only for the numbers 21, 31, 41, 51, 61, and 71. For all other compound numbers through 99, use a hyphen. **Un** becomes **une** before a feminine noun.

trente et un hommes (*31 men*)

trente et une femmes (*31 women*)

✔ **Quatre-vingts** and the plural **cents** drop the –s before another number but not before another noun.

quatre-vingt-trois (deux cent trois) pages (*83 [203] pages*)

but

quatre-vingts (deux cents) pages (*80 [200] pages*)

✔ The indefinite article **un/une** does not precede **cent** and **mille. Million, milliard** (*billion*), and **billion** (*trillion*) are nouns. They are preceded by **un** (or another number) and are followed by **de** before another noun.

Cent (mille) planètes (*100 [1,000] planets*)

Un million de planètes (*1,000,000 planets*)

Deux milliards de dollars (*2 billion dollars*)

✔ **Mille** does not change in the plural.

Six mille étoiles (*6,000 stars*)

✔ **Mille** is often written as **mil** in dates.

Il est né en deux mil douze. (*He was born in 2012.*)

With numerals and decimals, French uses commas where English uses periods, and vice versa.

English	French
6,000	6.000
0.75	0,75
$14.99	$14,99

Expressing ordinal numbers

You use *ordinal numbers* — those used to express numbers in a series — far less frequently than cardinal numbers, but they still have some very important applications in everyday life. Table 1-1 presents the French ordinal numbers.

Table 1-1	French Ordinal Numbers	
English Ordinal	**French Ordinal**	**Abbreviation**
1st	premier, première	1er, 1ère
2nd	deuxième, second(e)	2e
3rd	troisième	3e
4th	quatrième	4e
5th	cinquième	5e
6th	sixième	6e
7th	septième	7e
8th	huitième	8e
9th	neuvième	9e
10th	dixième	10e

The following list outlines what you must remember when using ordinal numbers in French.

- ✔ **Second(e)** usually replaces **deuxième** in a series that does not go beyond two.

  son deuxième livre (*his second book* – there are more than two)

  son second livre (*his second book* – he wrote only two)

- ✔ **Premier** and **second** are the only ordinal numbers to have a feminine form: première and seconde, respectively.

  le premier garçon (*the first boy*)

> **la première fille** *(the first girl)*
>
> **la seconde pièce** *(the second play)*
>
> **le second acte** *(the second act)*

- ✔ Except for **premier** and **second,** ordinal numbers are formed by adding **–ième** to the cardinal numbers. Silent **e** is dropped: **quatrième.**

- ✔ Note the **u** added to **cinquième** and the **f** that changes to **v** in **neuvième.**

Setting the Date

Knowing French calendar words and how to say what day it is makes it easier for you to make appointments, break dates, and plan outings.

Naming the days of the week

The days of the week end in **-di,** except for Sunday, which begins with those two letters.

In French, the week starts on Monday, not Sunday, and you don't capitalize the names of days. Here are **les jours de la semaine** *(the days of the week)*:

- ✔ **lundi** *(Monday)*
- ✔ **mardi** *(Tuesday)*
- ✔ **mercredi** *(Wednesday)*
- ✔ **jeudi** *(Thursday)*
- ✔ **vendredi** *(Friday)*
- ✔ **samedi** *(Saturday)*
- ✔ **dimanche** *(Sunday)*

If you want to know what day of the week it is, ask **Quel jour sommes-nous?** or **Quel jour est-ce?** You can answer such a question with any of the following phrases followed by the day of the week: **Nous sommes, On est,** or **C'est.**

> **C'est mardi.** *(It's Tuesday.)*

To say that something happens on a certain day, you just use that day with no preposition or article.

> **Je vais à la banque lundi.** (*I am going to the bank on Monday.*)

To say that something generally happens on a certain day, you use the definite article.

> **Je vais à la banque le vendredi.** (*I go to the bank on Fridays.*)

Here are some other useful words related to days and weeks:

- ✔ **hier** (*yesterday*)
- ✔ **aujourd'hui** (*today*)
- ✔ **demain** (*tomorrow*)
- ✔ **la semaine dernière (passée)** (*last week*)
- ✔ **cette semaine** (*this week*)
- ✔ **la semaine prochaine** (*next week*)

Using the months of the year

You need to know the names of the months in French when writing a letter or making a date. This list shows you the months of the year, which, like the days of the week, aren't capitalized.

- ✔ **janvier** (*January*)
- ✔ **février** (*February*)
- ✔ **mars** (*March*)
- ✔ **avril** (*April*)
- ✔ **mai** (*May*)
- ✔ **juin** (*June*)
- ✔ **juillet** (*July*)
- ✔ **août** (*August*)

> ✔ **septembre** *(September)*
>
> ✔ **octobre** *(October)*
>
> ✔ **novembre** *(November)*
>
> ✔ **décembre** *(December)*

To say that something happened or will happen in a given month, use the preposition **en.**

> **J'ai acheté ma voiture en juin.** *(I bought my car in June.)*

Giving the date

Every event takes place on a particular date. So if you want to invite or if you are invited, you need to know how to express the date. The first thing to know is the question:

> **Quelle est la date (d'aujourd'hui)?** *(What's the date [today]?)*

To answer, you can say **Nous sommes, On est,** or **C'est** followed by **le** + *cardinal number* + *month* + *year (optional).* Notice that the day comes before the month and its number has to be preceded by the definite article **le.** For example:

> **C'est (lundi) le 3 [trois] mai.** *(It's [Monday] May 3.)*

> **On est le 22 [vingt-deux] février 2010 [deux mil dix].** *(It's February 22, 2010.)*

Use a cardinal number to say the date in French except when you're talking about the first day of the month. For that you use **premier.**

> **C'est le 1ᵉʳ [premier] décembre.** *(It's December 1st.)*

In French, when dates are written as numbers, they follow the sequence day/month/year, which may prove confusing to English speakers — especially for dates below the 12th of the month. You write *February 9th* as 2/9 in English, but in French it's 9/2.

Telling Time

When writing and speaking French, knowing and telling the time is an important concept to master especially when you have an appointment or a train to catch. The first thing you need to know is how to ask what time it is: **Quelle heure est-il?** The response may be one of the following:

> **Il est midi (minuit).** *(It's noon [midnight].)*
>
> **Il est . . . heure(s).** *(It's . . . o'clock.)* (use *heure* only for 1 o'clock)

In France, the 24-hour system is used in public announcements and timetables. So the morning hours are 1 to 12, and the afternoon and evening hours (expressed in full numbers) are 13 to 24. To convert back to a 12-hour clock, subtract 12 from any time greater than 12.

To express the time after the hour (but before half past the hour), the number of minutes is added. To express the time for the second half of the hour, the number of minutes is subtracted from the next hour. Use *et* *(and)* only with **quart et demi(e).** You can also express time numerically (as shown in the third example here).

> **Il est une heure et demie.** *(It's 1:30.)*
>
> **Il est cinq heures moins vingt.** *(It's 4:40.)*
>
> **Il est quatre heures quarante.** *(It's 4:40.)*

If you want to ask at what time an event is taking place, use **à quelle heure.**

> **À quelle heure est la téléconférence?** *([At] What time is the conference call?)*

To answer, you just start with that event and add **à** and the time.

> **La téléconférence est à midi.** *(The conference call is at noon.)*

The following chart shows how to express time after and before the hour.

Time	French
1:00	**une heure**
2:05	**deux heures cinq**
3:10	**trois heures dix**
4:15	**quatre heures et quart**
5:20	**cinq heures vingt**
6:25	**six heures vingt-cinq**
7:30	**sept heures et demie**
7:35	**huit heures moins vingt-cinq** or **sept heures trente-cinq**
8:40	**neuf heures moins vingt** or **huit heures quarante**
9:45	**dix heures moins le quart** or **neuf heures quarante-cinq**
10:50	**onze heures moins dix** or **dix heures cinquante**
10:55	**onze heures moins cinq** or **dix heures cinquante-cinq**
noon	**midi**
midnight	**minuit**

To express half past noon or midnight, use **demi.**

> **Il est midi (minuit) et demi.** *(It's half past noon [midnight].)*

Demie is used to express *half past* with all other times.

> **Il est trois heures et demie.** *(It's 3:30.)*

In French, an **h** (short for **heures**) is used where English uses a colon.

> **14h00** *(2:00 p.m.)*
>
> **8h30** *(8:30 a.m.)*

Reviewing the Parts of Speech

Language is made up of parts of speech — nouns, verbs, adjectives, and so on. Each of these building blocks has its own function and rules, and understanding them is key to using them correctly, particularly with a foreign language. If you don't know the difference between the parts of speech in English, you probably won't understand them in French, either.

Identifying things with nouns and articles

Nouns are people, places, things, and ideas. They're the concrete and abstract things in your sentences, the *who* and the *what* that are doing something or having something done to them. Take a look at the example:

> **<u>Marie</u> veut vraiment visiter les <u>musées</u> célèbres.** *(<u>Marie</u> really wants to visit the famous <u>museums</u>.)*

Unlike English nouns, all French nouns have a gender (masculine or feminine) and a number (singular or plural). All words you use to qualify or describe a noun must agree with the noun with respect to gender. We discuss this subject in more detail in Chapter 2.

An article is a very particular part of speech. You can use it only with a noun. French has three kinds of articles:

- ✔ Definite articles: **le, la, l', les** *(the)*
- ✔ Indefinite articles: **un, une** *(a/an)*, **des** *(some)*
- ✔ Partitive articles: **du, de la, de l', des** *(some)*

Replacing with pronouns

Pronouns are easy to understand; they replace nouns. That is, pronouns also refer to people, places, things, and ideas, but they let you avoid repeating the same words over and over. The following list outlines the pronouns we discuss in this book.

✔ *Subject pronouns* (see Chapter 3) are followed by the verb expressing the main action in the sentence (*I, you, he, she, it, we, they*).

Tu es sympathique. *(<u>You</u> are nice.)*

✔ *Interrogative pronouns* (see Chapter 6) ask a question (*who, which, what, and so on*).

Qui est-ce? *(<u>Who</u> is that?)*

✔ *Direct object pronouns* (see Chapter 2) replace direct object nouns; they answer who or what the subject is acting upon. The direct object pronouns are **me, te, le, la, nous, vous**, and **les**.

Il te voit. *(He sees <u>you</u>.)*

✔ *Indirect object pronouns* (see Chapter 2) replace indirect object nouns; they explain to or for whom something is done. They include **me, te, lui, nous, vous**, and **leur**.

Il lui a écrit. *(He wrote to <u>her</u>.)*

✔ *Adverbial pronouns* (see Chapter 2) **y** and **en** have various applications that are explained in more detail in Chapter 2.

✔ *Reflexive pronouns* (see Chapter 3) show that the subject is acting upon itself (**me, te, se, nous**, and **vous**).

Elle se regarde dans le miroir. *(She is looking at <u>herself</u> in the mirror.)*

✔ *Prepositional pronouns,* also used as stress pronouns (see Chapter 5), are used after prepositions: **moi, toi, lui, elle, nous, vous, eux**, and **elles**.

Ils vont au cinéma sans moi. *(They're going to the movies without <u>me</u>.)*

Moving along with verbs

A verb is a part of speech that shows an action or a state of being. In French, as in English, verbs change from their infinitive form (in other words, they're *conjugated*) as follows:

✔ To agree with the person performing the action (I, you, he, she, it, we, they).

✔ To indicate the time when the action was performed (past, present, future).

✔ To indicate the mood (subjunctive, imperative, conditional, indicative) of the action.

French verbs are classified by how they're conjugated:

✔ Regular verbs: **-er** verbs, **-ir** verbs, and **-re** verbs

✔ Spelling-change verbs

✔ Irregular verbs

✔ Reflexive verbs

The *infinitive* of the verb is its "raw" form — its "to" form before it's conjugated: **danser** *(to dance),* **finir** *(to finish),* **répondre** *(to answer).* Regular infinitives in French have three different endings, and you conjugate them according to these endings **(-er, -ir,** and **-re).** We give you lots more information about verbs in Chapters 3, 7, 8, and 9.

Modifying with adjectives

Adjectives may be flowery words that describe nouns.

> **Je veux vraiment aller en France et visiter les musées célèbres.** *(I really want to go to France and visit the <u>famous</u> museums.)*

But adjectives are not only descriptive; they come in many other useful varieties:

✔ Demonstrative adjectives: **ce, cet, cette** *(this, that),* **ces** *(these, those)*

✔ Interrogative adjectives: **quel, quelle, quels, quelles** *(which)*

✔ Possessive adjectives: **mon** *(my),* **ton** *(your),* **son** *(his/ her/its)*

Unlike English adjectives, French adjectives have masculine, feminine, singular, and plural forms so that they can agree with nouns. (Chapter 4 tells you lots of other interesting details about adjectives.)

Qualifying with adverbs

Adverbs modify verbs, adjectives, and other adverbs. In the example sentence, *really* modifies the verb *want.*

> **Je veux <u>vraiment</u> aller en France et visiter les musées célèbres.** *(I <u>really</u> want to go to France and visit the famous museums.)*

English adverbs often end in *-ly* and indicate how the action of a verb is occurring: happily, quickly, rudely. Most of these words are *adverbs of manner.* The other kinds of adverbs are

- Adverbs of frequency: **jamais** *(never),* **souvent** *(often)*
- Adverbs of place: **ici** *(here),* **partout** *(everywhere)*
- Adverbs of quantity: **beaucoup de** *(a lot),* **peu de** *(few)*
- Adverbs of time: **avant** *(before),* **demain** *(tomorrow)*
- Interrogative adverbs: **quand** *(when),* **où** *(where)*

Read Chapter 4 thoroughly to understand more about French adverbs.

Connecting with prepositions

A *preposition* is the part of speech you put in front of a noun or pronoun to show the relationship between that word and another word or phrase. Prepositions tell you how verbs and nouns fit together. Prepositions may be one word *(to, at, about)* or part of a group of words *(next to, in front of, on top of).*

> **Je veux vraiment aller <u>en</u> France et visiter les musées célèbres.** *(I really want to go <u>to</u> France and visit the famous museums.)*

Prepositions are not like a list of vocabulary that you can just memorize. Instead, they're grammatical terms with various functions that you have to study and practice. Chapter 5 explains all about prepositions.

Chapter 2

Narrowing the Gender Gap

- -

In This Chapter

▶ Getting specific with definite articles

▶ Being general with indefinite articles

▶ Describing with adjectives

▶ Choosing a gender

▶ Expressing possession

▶ Using object pronouns

- -

*I*n French, all nouns have a gender, which makes more of a difference than you can possibly imagine. A noun's gender determines which form of articles, adjectives, pronouns, and sometimes past participles you have to use, so knowing the gender is vital to speaking and writing French.

In this chapter, we help you to correctly mark the gender of a noun by using definite articles (which express *the*), indefinite articles (which express *a, an,* or *some*), demonstrative adjectives (which express *this, that, these,* or *those*), or partitive articles (which express *some* or part of a thing). You can read up on two different ways to show possession of things, how to replace direct and indirect object nouns with their respective pronouns, and how to use the adverbial pronouns **y** and **en.**

Specifying with Definite Articles

Definite articles indicate that the noun they're presenting is specific. In English, the definite article is *the*. French definite articles tell you that the noun is masculine or feminine, singular or plural.

Distinguishing the definite articles

French features three distinct definite articles that usually correspond to *the* in English.

The following table lists the French definite articles. Note that if the noun is plural, the article is **les,** no matter what gender the noun is.

	Masculine	*Feminine*
Singular	**le (l')**	**la (l')**
Plural	**les**	**les**

Le livre est intéressant. *(The book is interesting.)*

You use the French definite article to talk about the general sense of a noun. Note that in the example that follows, the definite article is not used in English.

J'aime le chocolat. *(I like chocolate.)*

If a singular noun begins with a vowel or mute *h*, the definite article **le** or **la** contracts to **l':**

l'ami *(the friend)*

l'eau *(the water)*

l'homme *(the man)*

Using definite articles

You may come across many instances in French where you use the definite article even though you may or may not use it in English. The rules in the following list show how you use the definite articles in French:

✔ With nouns in a general or abstract sense:

L'amour est divin. *(Love is divine.)*

J'aime le vin blanc. *(I like white wine.)*

✔ With names of languages (except after the verb **parler** and after the prepositions **de** and **en**):

J'aime le français. *(I like French.)*

Où est mon livre de français? *(Where's my French book?)*

Écris-moi en français. *(Write to me in French.)*

✔ With parts of the body (when the possessor is clear) in place of the possessive adjective:

Je me lave les cheveux. *(I wash my hair.)*

✔ With titles and ranks when you aren't addressing the person:

Le docteur Caron est prêt. *(Doctor Caron is ready.)*

but

Bonjour, Docteur Caron. *(Hello, Doctor Caron.)*

✔ With last names:

Les Ricard habitent Paris. *(The Ricards live in Paris.)*

✔ With days of the week in a plural sense:

Je ne travaille pas le samedi. *(I don't work on Sundays.)*

✔ With dates:

C'est le cinq mai. *(It's May 5th.)*

✔ With the names of many geographical locations, except after the preposition **en:**

La France est belle. *(France is beautiful.)*

but

Nous allons en France. *(We are going to France.)*

Contracting with definite articles

The preposition **à** can mean to, in, or at. When the preposition **à** is followed by a definite article, a contraction may have to be made. Table 2-1 explains two contractions: **à + le** and **à + les.**

Table 2-1	Combining Definite Articles with the Preposition à	
Preposition + Article	**Combination**	**Example**
à + le	au	**Je réponds au professeur.** *(I'm answering the professor.)*
à + la	à la	**Je réponds à la question.** *(I'm answering the question.)*
à + l'	à l'	**Je réponds à l'étudiant.** *(I'm answering the student.)*
à + les	aux	**Je réponds aux questions.** *(I'm answering the questions.)*

Generalizing with Indefinite Articles

An *indefinite article,* which usually expresses the English words *a, an,* or *some,* refers to persons or objects not specifically identified (such as "a boy" or "some books"). Just as with definite articles, indefinite articles can tell you whether a noun is masculine or feminine and singular or plural.

Three French indefinite articles correspond to *a, an,* and *one* in the singular and to *some* in the plural. The following table presents these articles.

	Masculine	*Feminine*
Singular	**un**	**une**
Plural	**des**	**des**

Here are some examples of the indefinite articles in action:

Elle a acheté un manteau. *(She bought an overcoat.)*

C'est une belle femme. *(She is a very beautiful woman.)*

Il me faut des crayons. *(I need some pencils.)*

Although "some" may be implicit in English, in French the indefinite article **des** must always be used:

> **J'ai des amis qui parlent français.** *(I have [some] friends who speak French.)*

As with definite articles, the indefinite article precedes the noun it modifies and agrees with that noun in number and gender.

When you negate a sentence with an indefinite article, the article changes to **de** (**d'** before a vowel), meaning *(not) any*.

> **J'ai des questions.** *(I have some questions.)*
>
> **Je n'ai pas de questions.** *(I don't have any questions.)*
>
> **Il n'y a pas d'excuse.** *(There's no excuse.)*

See Chapter 6 for more information about negation.

Understanding the Partitive

The partitive, which does not exist in English, expresses part of a whole and may be translated as *some* or *any* in English. The partitive is generally formed by combining **de** + the definite article as shown in the chart below.

Partitive	*Used before:*
du (de + le)	Masculine singular nouns beginning with consonant
de la	Feminine singular nouns beginning with a consonant
de l'	Any singular noun beginning with a vowel
des (de + les)	All plural nouns

Here are some examples using the partitive:

> **Il prend du café.** *(He drinks coffee.)*
>
> **Manges-tu de la viande?** *(Do you eat meat?)*

Avez-vous de l'argent? *(Do you have any money?)*

Je vais boire du lait. *(I'm going to drink some milk.)*

Although implicit in English, the partitive may not be omitted in French. In fact, it is repeated before each noun:

Veux-tu du jus ou de l'eau? *(Do you want juice or water?)*

In a negative sentence, the partitive is expressed by **de** without the definite article when it precedes the direct object of the verb or follows the expression **il n'y a pas** *(there isn't/ aren't)*:

Elle n'a pas de chance. *(She doesn't have any luck.)*

Il n'y a pas de problème. *(There isn't a problem.)*

With adverbs and nouns of quantity, and with expressions with **de, de** alone is used:

Elle a beaucoup d'amis. *(She has a lot of friends.)*

Je peux me passer de chocolat. *(I can do without chocolate.)*

The partitive is used to express some or a part of a whole, and the definite article is used with nouns in a general sense (to express an entire amount). Compare the following:

J'ai acheté du chocolat. *(I bought some chocolate.)*

J'ai acheté le chocolat. *(I bought the chocolate.)*

Je veux du gâteau. *(I want some cake.)*

Je veux le gâteau. *(I want the cake.)*

Using Demonstrative Adjectives

You use demonstrative adjectives when you want to talk about specific entities, such as *this, that, these,* or *those. Demonstrative adjectives* are used with nouns. The demonstrative adjective goes in front of a noun to indicate that you're referring to this or that particular noun. Like other French adjectives, demonstrative adjectives have different forms depending on the gender and number of the noun they precede. In addition, you use a special form with masculine singular nouns that begin with a vowel or mute *h* — see Table 2-2.

Table 2-2   Demonstrative Adjectives

Gender	Singular (This/That)	Plural (These/Those)
Masculine	ce	ces
Masculine + vowel	cet	ces
Feminine	cette	ces

Check out these examples:

Masculine: **Ce livre est intéressant.** *(This/That book is interesting.)*

Masculine + vowel: **Qui a écrit cet article?** *(Who wrote this/that article?)*

Masculine + mute: **Cet homme est grand.** *(This/That man is tall.)*

Feminine: **Cette maison est bleue.** *(This/That house is blue.)*

Ce, cet, and **cette** can all mean *this* or *that* — French doesn't have separate words to make this distinction. You can usually tell by context, but if not, you can add the suffixes **-ci** (*here*) and **-là** (*there*) to the end of the noun:

Ce livre-ci est intéressant. *(This book [here] is interesting.)*

Ce livre-là est stupide. *(That book [there] is stupid.)*

The plural demonstrative adjective **ces** can mean *these* or *those;* again, you can use **-ci** and **-là** to clarify, if necessary:

Ces maisons sont vertes. *(These/Those houses are green.)*

Ces maisons-ci sont grises. *(These houses [here] are gray.)*

Ces maisons-là sont jaunes. *(Those houses [there] are yellow.)*

French has only one plural demonstrative adjective. You use **ces** for all plurals: masculine, masculine + vowel/mute *h,* and feminine.

Taking the Guesswork out of Gender

French nouns are either masculine or feminine. Nouns that refer to males are always masculine, and nouns that refer to females are feminine, no matter their endings. You can't always be sure when it comes to places or things, though.

Learning the gender of nouns

Most nouns that refer to people have a logical gender. **Homme** *(man),* **garçon** *(boy),* and **serveur** *(waiter)* are masculine, and **femme** *(woman),* **fille** *(girl),* and **serveuse** *(waitress)* are feminine. In most cases, there's no way to just look at a word and know its gender — you have to memorize the gender of each word as you learn it.

The best way to remember the gender of nouns is to make sure your vocabulary lists include an indefinite article for each noun because these articles don't change in front of vowels.

Using the same noun for both genders

Nouns that refer to people often have a masculine "default" form that can be made feminine (see Table 2-3 for examples). Here's how to make the gender switch:

- ✔ To make most of these nouns feminine, just add **-e** to the end. For example, **un étudiant** *(male student)* becomes **une étudiante** *(female student).*

- ✔ If a masculine noun ends in **-en** or **-on,** add **-ne** for the feminine form: **Un pharmacien** *(pharmacist)* becomes **une pharmacienne.**

✔ Nouns that end in **-er** change to **-ère** for the feminine.

✔ Nouns that end in **-eur** changes to **-euse** or and **–teur** changes to **-trice.**

✔ Nouns that end in **-e** in the masculine form have no change for the feminine (other than in the article, which changes to **une, la,** or **de la**).

Table 2-3   Masculine and Feminine Nouns

English	Masculine	Feminine
lawyer	un avocat	une avocat**e**
electrician	un électrici**en**	une électrici**enne**
boss	un patr**on**	une patr**onne**
cashier	un caissi**er**	une caissi**ère**
salesperson	un vend**eur**	une vend**euse**
translator	un traduc**teur**	une traduc**trice**
tourist	un touris**te**	une touris**te**

A number of French nouns have only a masculine or a feminine form, regardless of the gender of the person they refer to.

The following nouns are always masculine:

✔ **un auteur** *(author)*

✔ **un bébé** *(baby)*

✔ **un charpentier** *(carpenter)*

✔ **un chef** *(chef, cook, chief, head)*

✔ **un écrivain** *(writer)*

✔ **un gouverneur** *(governor)*

✔ **un ingénieur** *(engineer)*

✔ **un maire** *(mayor)*

✔ **un médecin** *(doctor)*

✔ **un peintre** *(painter)*

✔ **un plombier** *(plumber)*

✔ **un poète** *(poet)*

✔ **un policier** *(police officer)*

✔ **un pompier** *(firefighter)*

✔ **un professeur** *(teacher)*

✔ **un témoin** *(witness)*

And these nouns are always feminine:

✔ **une connaissance** *(acquaintance)*

✔ **une idole** *(idol)*

✔ **une personne** *(person)*

✔ **une vedette** *(movie star)*

✔ **une victime** *(victim)*

Recognizing the gender of nouns

A few word endings usually indicate whether a noun is masculine or feminine. Table 2-4 provides a quick guide.

Table 2-4	Word Endings of Masculine and Feminine Nouns		
Ending	*Usually Masculine Noun*	*Ending*	*Usually Feminine Noun*
-acle	**le spectacle**	-ade*	**la limonade**
-age*	**le garage**	-ale	**la cathédrale**
-al	**le journal**	-ance	**l'enfance**
-eau*	**le bureau**	-ence	**la conférence**
-et	**le bracelet**	-ette	**la baguette**
-ier	**le dossier**	-ie	**la compagnie**
-isme	**le tourisme**	-ique	**la musique**
-ment	**le gouvernement**	-oire	**l'histoire**
		-sion	**l'excursion**
		-tion	**la portion**
		-ure	**la culture**

* Note these common exceptions:

> ✔ **le stade** *(the stadium)*
>
> ✔ **la page, la plage** *(the beach)*
>
> ✔ **l'eau (f.)** *(water)*
>
> ✔ **la peau** *(the skin)*

Pluralizing Nouns

In addition to masculine and feminine forms, most nouns also have singular and plural forms. Making a noun plural in French is very similar to making a noun plural in English. To make a noun plural, you usually just add an **-s:** changing **un livre** *(a book)* to **deux livres** *(two books)* and **la revue** *(the magazine)* to **les revues** *(the magazines).* The final **s** is silent, which means that the singular and plural forms of these nouns are pronounced the same way. But you can tell that the noun is plural because the article or number changes.

French often has masculine and feminine words for nouns referring to people, like **un ami** *(male friend)* and **une amie** *(female friend).* However, if you have a group of mixed masculine and feminine nouns, you always default to the masculine: **des amis.** The only time you can say **des amies** is when you're talking about a group of just girl friends, with not a single male in the bunch. The same idea applies if you're talking about one person whose gender you don't know, such as *one tourist —* if you don't know whether it's a man or woman, you always default to the masculine: **un touriste.**

This section explains how to form a plural when you can't simply add an **-s.**

Using x instead of s

Though most French nouns just add an **-s** for plurals, a few take an **-x** with or without some other letter changes/additions. These nouns always end in one of the following letter combinations, which let you know that **-x** marks the (plural) spot. See Table 2-5 for some examples.

Table 2-5		Plural Patterns		
English	*French Singular*	*Singular Ending*	*French Plural*	*Plural Ending*
work	le trav**ail**	-**ail**	les trav**aux**	-**aux**
newspaper	le journ**al**	-**al**	les journ**aux**	-**aux**
coat	le mant**eau**	-**eau**	les mant**eaux**	-**eaux**
jewel	le bij**ou**	-**ou***	les bij**oux**	-**oux**
game	le j**eu**	-**eu****	les j**eux**	-**eux**

* Six other nouns ending in **–ou** add **–x** in the plural: **les cailloux** *(the pebbles)*, **les choux** *(the cabbages)*, **les genoux** *(the knees)*, **les hiboux** *(the owls)*, **les joujoux** *(the toys)*, and **les poux** *(the lice)*. All other nouns ending in **–ou** add **–s** in the plural: **les trous** *(the holes)*.

** A common exception to this rule is **les pneus** *(the tires)*.

Irregular plurals

Some French nouns are irregular. When a noun ends in **-s, -x,** or **-z,** you don't add anything to make the word plural; the singular and plural forms are identical. To tell the difference between the singular and plural, you have to pay special attention to the article

> ✔ **le mois** (the month) becomes **les mois**
>
> ✔ **le prix** (the price) becomes **les prix**
>
> ✔ **le nez** (the nose) becomes **les nez**

Do not add –s in the plural for family names.

A few French nouns have irregular plurals; see Table 2-6 to memorize the most common ones.

Table 2-6	Irregular Plurals	
English	*French Singular*	*French Plural*
eye	**un œil**	**des yeux**
ma'am	**madame**	**mesdames**
miss	**mademoiselle**	**mesdemoiselles**
sir	**monsieur**	**messieurs**
sky	**le ciel**	**les cieux**

The plurals of **madame, mademoiselle,** and **monsieur** add an **-s** at the end of the word, which is normal, but they also change from the singular possessive adjective (**mon** or **ma,** which means *my*) at the beginning to the plural possessive adjective (**mes,** which means *my*). See the section "Using possessive adjectives" later in this chapter for more info.

Compound nouns

The plural of compound nouns can be a little tricky. The most common are shown in this chart:

Singular	*Plural*
l'après midi (m.) *(afternoon)*	**les après-midi**
le chef-d'oeuvre *(masterpiece)*	**les chefs-d'oeuvre**
la grand-mère *(grandmother)*	**les grands-mères**
le grand-père *(grandfather)*	**les grands-pères**
le gratte-ciel *(skyscraper)*	**les gratte-ciel**
l'hors d'oeuvre *(appetizer)*	**les hors-d'oeuvre**
le rendez-vous *(appointment)*	**les rendez-vous**

Plural nouns

Some nouns are used mainly in the plural. The most common are:

✔ **les ciseaux (m.)** *(scissors)*

✔ **les gens (m. or f.)** *(people)*

  ✔ **les lunettes (f.)** *(eyeglasses)*

  ✔ **les mathématiques (f.)** *(mathematics)*

  ✔ **les vacances (f.)** *(vacation)*

Confirming Possession

French has different ways to express ownership: by using the preposition **de** and by using possessive adjectives. This section explains both so you can make sure that everyone knows whose is whose.

Utilizing de

In English, when you want to say that something belongs to someone or something, you use an apostrophe: either *'s* or *s'*. French is completely different. You have to reverse the order of the nouns and join them with the preposition **de.** In other words, start with the thing that's owned and then add **de** and the owner.

> **la maison de Michel** *(Michel's house;* Literally: *the house of Michel)*

> **les chaussures de Sylvie** *(Sylvie's shoes;* Literally: *the shoes of Sylvie)*

> **l'idée de l'étudiant** *(the student's idea;* Literally: *the idea of the student)*

> **la chambre de mes sœurs** *(my sisters' room;* Literally: *the room of my sisters)*

Using possessive adjectives

Possessive adjectives go in front of nouns to tell you who or what those nouns belong to. In French there are different forms for masculine, feminine, singular, and plural possessive adjectives. In order to use the correct one, you need to consider the gender and number of the noun possessed. To say *my house,* you need to remember that **maison** *(house)* is feminine and singular, so you want to use the feminine singular form of the adjective (**ma**): **ma maison.** See Table 2-7 for the different forms of French possessive adjectives.

Table 2-7	Possessive Adjectives		
English	*Masculine*	*Feminine*	*Plural*
my	**mon**	**ma**	**mes**
your (**tu** form)	**ton**	**ta**	**tes**
his/her/its	**son**	**sa**	**ses**
our	**notre**	**notre**	**nos**
your (**vous** form)	**votre**	**votre**	**vos**
their	**leur**	**leur**	**leurs**

Singular subjects

The possessive adjectives for first-, second-, and third-person singular subjects have three forms, depending on the gender, number, and first letter of the noun they're used with — see Table 2-8.

In English, the choice of *his* or *her* depends on the gender of the person/thing that possesses the object: *Tom's sister* becomes *his sister,* and *Jane's sister* becomes *her sister.* In French, the gender of the thing possessed determines whether to say **son** or **sa:** *His sister* and *her sister* are both translated as **sa sœur** because **sœur** is feminine. Likewise, *his brother* and *her brother* are both translated as **son frère** because **frère** is masculine. But if you really need to be clear about whether you mean *his* or *her,* you can add **à lui** or **à elle: C'est son frère à lui** *(It's his brother)* and **C'est son frère à elle** *(It's her brother).*

You can use **ma, ta,** and **sa** only with a feminine noun that begins with a consonant. When a feminine noun begins with a vowel or mute h, you have to use the masculine adjective (**mon, ton,** or **son**).

Table 2-8	Singular-Subject Possessive Adjectives		
Masculine	*Feminine*	*Feminine before a Vowel*	*Plural*
mon frère *(my brother)*	ma sœur *(my sister)*	mon amie *(my friend)*	mes parents *(my parents)*
ton frère *(your brother)*	ta sœur *(your sister)*	ton amie *(your friend)*	tes parents *(your parents)*
son frère *(his/ her brother)*	sa sœur *(his/ her sister)*	son amie *(his/ her friend)*	ses amis *(his/ her parents)*

Plural subjects

First-, second-, and third-person plural subjects have only two forms of the possessive adjective: singular and plural. Whether the noun being possessed is masculine or feminine — or whether it starts with a consonant or vowel — doesn't matter. See Table 2-9.

Table 2-9	Plural-Subject Possessive Adjectives
Singular	*Plural*
notre père *(our father)*	nos amis *(our friends)*
votre père *(your father)*	vos amis *(your friends)*
leur père *(their father)*	leurs amis *(their friends)*

Possessive adjectives are not used with parts of the body. (See Chapter 3 for more on reflexive verbs.)

Il se lave les mains. *(He washes his hands.)*

Possessive adjectives do not have to agree with the subject of the sentence.

J'aime sa soeur. *(I love his sister.)*

Substituting with Object Pronouns

Direct object pronouns replace direct object nouns, and indirect object pronouns replace indirect object nouns. Despite the objectified nature of the word, objects aren't always just things like books and trees — they can, and often do, refer to people and animals. This section spells out how to use direct object and indirect object pronouns so everyone clearly knows what he or she is writing or talking about.

Coping with direct object pronouns

To use a direct object pronoun, you first need to be able to identify the direct object noun. Do this by asking whom or what the subject is acting upon. For example, in the sentence **Lise connaît les athlètes** *(Lise knows the athletes),* Lise is the subject of the sentence. To find the direct object, you'd ask, "Whom does Lise know?" **Athlètes** is the object — the people she knows. You can replace the direct objects **les athlètes** with a direct object pronoun. When you choose a direct object pronoun, you have to consider the gender and number of the noun you're replacing. Unlike in English, French direct object pronouns precede the verb.

Table 2-10 lists the direct object pronouns in French.

Table 2-10	Direct Object Pronouns		
Singular Pronouns	*Meaning*	*Plural Pronouns*	*Meaning*
me (m')	*me*	nous	*us*
te (t')	*you* (familiar)	vous	*you* (polite)
le (l')	*him, it*	les	*them*
la (l')	*her, it*	les	*them*

Here are some example sentences that show how you use French direct object pronouns:

> **Lise connaît les Lambert.** *(Lise knows the Lamberts.)*
>
> **Lise les connaît.** *(Lise knows them.)*
>
> **Mon frère déteste la natation.** *(My brother hates swimming.)*
>
> **Mon frère la déteste.** *(My brother hates it.)*
>
> **Je vous aime.** *(I love you.)*

Me, te, le, and la become m', t', and l' whenever they precede a vowel, a mute h, or the adverbial pronouns y and en.

In the past tense (the passé composé), the past participle must agree in number and gender (add **-e** for feminine, **-s** for masculine plural, and **-es** for feminine plural) with the preceding direct object nouns and pronouns. (See Chapter 7 for more on the passé composé.)

> **J'aime la robe que tu as achetée.** *(I like the dress you bought.)*
>
> **Il a trouvé les journaux.** *(He found the newspapers.)*
>
> **Il les a trouvés.** *(He found them.)*
>
> **Elle a perdue ses clefs.** *(She lost her keys.)*
>
> **Elle les a perdues.** *(She lost them.)*

Handling indirect object pronouns

Indirect object nouns or *pronouns* refer only to people (and to beloved pets); they answer the question "To or for whom is the subject doing something?" And just as with direct object pronouns, indirect object pronouns generally are placed before the conjugated verb. For example:

> **Je lui écris un e-mail.** *(I'm writing [to] him/her an e-mail.)*
>
> **Il nous achète une voiture.** *(He is buying [for] us a car.)*

Table 2-11 presents the indirect object pronouns in French.

Table 2-11	**French Indirect Object Pronouns**		
Singular Pronouns	**Meaning**	**Plural Pronouns**	**Meaning**
me	*(to/for) me*	**nous**	*to/for us*
te	*(to/for) you* (familiar)	**vous**	*to/for you* (polite)
lui	*to/for him, her*	**leur**	*to/for them*

Note that the indirect object **leur** should not to be confused with the possessive adjective **leur/leurs,** which we discuss earlier in the chapter.

Elle leur parle. *(She's talking to them.)*

Je lui achète des livres. *(I'm buying [for] her some books.)*

Lui is the indirect object pronoun for both men and women:

Il téléphone à David. Il lui téléphone. *(He's calling David. He's calling him.)*

Je parle à ma mère. Je lui parle. *(I'm talking to my mother. I'm talking to her.)*

A clue that may indicate that you need an indirect object pronoun is the use of the preposition *à* **(au, à la,** or **aux),** which means *to* or *for,* followed by the name of or reference to a person.

Although you may use the prepositions *to* and *for* in English, you omit these prepositions in French sentences before an indirect object pronoun.

Je t'achète un cadeau. *(I'm buying a present for you; I'm buying you a present.)*

Ils m'écrivent. *(They are writing to me; They are writing me.)*

Eliminating confusion

Some verbs that would seem to take an indirect object in French actually take a direct object. The most common are:

- **attendre** *(to wait for)*
- **écouter** *(to listen to)*
- **chercher** *(to look for)*
- **payer** *(to pay for a thing)*
- **regarder** *(to look at)*

Here are some examples:

Il attend Anne. Il l'attend. *(He waits for her.)*

Nous écoutons le prof. Nous l'écoutons. *(We listen to him.)*

Sa mère paie la voiture. Sa mère la paie. *(His mother pays for it.)*

but

> **Sa mère lui paie la voiture.** *(His mother pays for the car for him.)*

Some verbs (those followed by the preposition **à**) that would seem to take a direct object in French actually take an indirect object. The most common are:

- ✔ **desobéir à** *(to disobey)*
- ✔ **obéir à** *(to obey)*
- ✔ **rendre visite à** *(to visit people)*
- ✔ **répondre à** *(to answer a person)*
- ✔ **ressembler à** *(to resemble)*
- ✔ **téléphoner à** *(to phone, call)*

Here are some examples:

> **J'obéis à mes parents. Je leur obéis.** *(I obey my parents. I obey them.)*

> **Elle répond à Luc. Elle lui répond.** *(She answers Luc. She answers him.)*

Figuring Out Adverbial Pronouns

Adverbial pronouns may replace a prepositional phrase or a noun that follows a number or an adverb of quantity. This section gives you the lowdown on the adverbial pronouns **y** and **en** and how to use them correctly.

Using y

You can use the adverbial pronoun **y** to replace prepositions that show location, such as **à, chez, dans,** and **en** + [a place] to express "there." The adverbial pronoun **y** goes in exactly the same place as direct and indirect object pronouns:

> **Je vais à la plage. J'y vais.** *(I'm going to the beach. I'm going there.)*

Elle passe deux jours en France. Elle y passe deux jours.
(She is spending two days in France. She is spending two days there.)

You can also use **y** to replace **à** + [a noun] with verbs that require the preposition **à:**

Je réponds à la lettre. J'y réponds. *(I answer the letter. I answer it.)*

Ils restent à la maison. Ils y restent. *(They stay at the house. They stay there.)*

 The indirect object tells you to or for whom something is being done, but **y** tells you what something is being done to. In French, indirect object pronouns can replace only people; you have to replace places and things with the adverbial pronoun **y:**

Je pense à l'amour. J'y pense. *(I'm thinking about love. I'm thinking about it.)*

Nous obéissons aux lois. Nous y obéissons. *(We obey the laws. We obey them.)*

but

Nous obéissons à nos parents. Nous leur obéissons. *(We obey our parents. We obey them.)*

Understanding en

The adverbial pronoun **en** usually translates to *some of it/them, of it/them, about it/them, from it/them,* or *from there.* The word order for **en** is the same as for object pronouns and the adverbial pronoun **y.** You can use **en** to replace

✔ **De** + noun

Je viens de New York. J'en viens. *(I come from New York. I come from there.)*

✔ Partitive article **du, de la,** or **des** + noun

Elle boit du café. Elle en boit. *(She drinks coffee. She drinks some.)*

✔ A noun after a number

Il a deux voitures. Il en a deux. *(He has two cars. He has two of them.)*

✔ An expression of quantity

J'ai assez d'argent. J'en ai assez. *(I have enough money. I have enough.)*

En replaces de + noun

With the preposition **de** and the partitive article (**du, de la, de l'**, or **des**), **en** replaces the article as well as the noun following it:

Je veux des fraises. J'en veux. *(I want some strawberries. I want some [of them].)*

En with numbers and nouns/adverbs of quantity

When you use **en** with a number, a noun, or an adverb of quantity, it replaces only the noun — you still need to put the number/noun/or adverb after the verb.

Il a trois voitures. Il en a trois. *(He has three cars. He has three [of them].)*

J'ai acheté une douzaine de livres. J'en ai acheté une douzaine. *(I bought a dozen books. I bought a dozen [of them].)*

Avez-vous beaucoup de temps? En avez-vous beaucoup ? *(Do you have a lot of time? Do you have a lot [of it]?)*

En is always expressed in French even if it is not expressed in English.

As-tu des problémes? *(Do you have problems?)*

Oui, J'en ai. *(Yes, I do [have some].)*

Placing Object Pronouns

How do you decide where to place a direct or indirect object pronoun or an adverbial pronoun in a French sentence? Generally, you place these pronouns before the conjugated verb.

Je t'aime. *(I love you.)*

> **Me prêtes-tu ta chemise?** *(Will you lend me your shirt?)*
>
> **Elle n'y va pas.** *(She isn't going there.)*
>
> **Nous en avons assez.** *(We have enough.)*

In sentences with two verbs (conjugated verb + infinitive) that follow one subject, place the object pronoun before the verb of which it is the object, usually the infinitive. (For more about verbs see Chapter 3.)

> **Veux-tu le faire?** *(Do you want to do it?)*
>
> **Je veux le faire.** *(I want to do it.)*
>
> **Ne veux-tu pas le faire?** *(Don't you want to do it?)*
>
> **Je ne veux pas le faire.** *(I don't want to do it.)*

In an affirmative command (see Chapter 9), the word order is different. Like reflexive pronouns (see Chapter 3), direct object pronouns follow the verb and are attached to it with hyphens; in addition, **me** changes to **moi** and **te** changes to **toi** respectively.

> **Trouvez-le.** *(Find it.)*
>
> **Écoute-moi!** *(Listen to me!)*

In a negative command, the pronoun precedes the verb.

> **Ne les cherche pas.** *(Don't look for them.)*
>
> **N'y va pas.** *(Don't go there.)*

Doing Double Time with Object Pronouns

The word order of pronouns in French is non-negotiable: Pronouns have to go in a certain order.

Object and adverbial pronouns, as well as reflexive pronouns (see Chapter 3), all go in the same place: in front of a conjugated verb or an infinitive — except in an affirmative command. Object and adverbial pronouns go in front of a verb, but in which order? This section clarifies the order.

Lining up: Standard pronoun order

Using any two object, adverbial, or reflexive pronouns together requires a very specific word order. Here's the order before a verb:

me, te, se, nous, vous → **le, la, les** → **lui, leur** → **y** → **en**

Coincidentally, before a verb, the pronouns **le, la, les,** and **lui** and **leur** are always placed in alphabetical order.

Check out the following examples of correctly placed pronouns:

> **Il m'a donné le livre. Il me l'a donné.** *(He gave me the book. He gave it to me.)*

> **Elle nous en parle.** *(She's talking to us about it.)*

> **Je vais le lui montrer.** *(I'm going to show it to him.)*

> **Il y en a trois.** *(There are three [of them].)*

Using pronouns in affirmative commands

In an affirmative command, the pronouns follow the verb and are joined to it with hyphens; here's the slightly different double-pronoun order that applies after the verb:

le, la, les → **moi, toi, lui, nous, vous, leur** → **y** → **en**

The pronouns **me** and **te** change to **moi** and **toi** respectively in affirmative commands (see Chapter 3). The important change is that the direct objects **le, la,** and **les** now come first instead of second.

After a verb, the pronouns **le, la, les, lui,** and **leur** are still always placed in alphabetical order.

> **Donnez-nous-en.** *(Give us some.)*

> **Va-t'en!** *(Go away!)*

> **Montrez-le-lui**. *(Show it to him.)*

Chapter 3

It's Happening in the Present

*I*n French, you use the present tense in everyday conversation. In fact, it's the building block in forming sentences and expressing thoughts. In French, the present tense is important because the stem of other tenses and moods, such as the imperfect and the subjunctive, are derived from it.

In this chapter, we classify the three regular types of verbs; discuss verbs with spelling changes; explain reflexive verbs; and show you verbs that are completely irregular.

Recognizing Types of Verbs

A good way to remember various verb conjugations is by classifying the verbs. The following four classifications help you identify the type of verb and enable you to conjugate it correctly.

> ✔ **Regular verbs:** These verbs follow the regular conjugation rules for **-er, -ir,** and **-re** verbs, which are the three groups of regular verbs.

✔ **Spelling-change verbs:** Some French verbs undergo spelling changes. These verbs may double their interior consonants, add an accent to a mute e **(è),** add an **e** after g, or change c to **ç.**

✔ **Irregular verbs:** These verbs have an irregular conjugation and don't follow a specific pattern like regular verbs do.

✔ **Reflexive verbs:** You use these verbs when you do something to yourself. The action reflects back to the subject of the sentence.

Choosing Subject Pronouns

A *subject pronoun* is a word used in place of a subject noun. *I, you, he, she, it, we,* and *they* are the English subject pronouns. They indicate who or what is performing the action, and they dictate the form of the verb you must use. In English, he *shops,* but they *shop.* The French subject pronouns are shown in Table 3-1.

Table 3-1		French Subject Pronouns		
Person	**Singular**	**Meaning**	**Plural**	**Meaning**
1st person	**je**	*I*	**nous**	*we*
2nd person	**tu**	*you* (familiar)	**vous** (polite)	*you*
3rd person	**il**	*he*	**ils**	*they*
	elle	*she*	**elles**	*they*
	on	*one, you, we, they, people*		

Unlike the English subject pronoun *I,* which is always capitalized, the French pronoun **je** is capitalized only at the beginning of a sentence and becomes **j'** before a vowel or a mute h. Here are some examples:

Je parle français. *(I speak French.)*

Tu sais, je ne parle pas espagnol. *(You know, I don't speak Spanish.)*

J'aime le tennis. *(I like tennis.)*

Tu versus vous

Tu and **vous** both mean *you,* but French distinguishes between different kinds of you:

- **Tu** is singular and informal. You use it only when you're talking to one person you know well — such as a family member, friend, classmate, or colleague — or to a child or animal.

- **Vous** can be singular (formal) or plural (formal and informal). You have to use it:

  - When talking to one person you don't know or to whom you wish to show respect, such as your teacher, doctor, or boss.

  - When you're talking to more than one person, whether or not you know them.

If you're not sure whether to use **tu** or **vous,** be respectful and opt for **vous.**

Il versus elle, and on

Il and **elle** mean *he* and *she,* respectively. Both **il** and **elle** can mean *it* when referring to a thing. To say *it,* you have to know the gender of the noun before you use either pronoun. (See Chapter 2 for details on noun gender).

Il a deux sœurs. *(He has two sisters.)*

Je vois mon livre. Il est sur la table. *(I see my book. It's on the table.)*

Elle veut travailler ici. *(She wants to work here.)*

Je vois la voiture. Elle est dans la rue. *(I see the car. It's in the street.)*

On is an indefinite pronoun that literally means *one.* But **on** can also mean *you, we* (informally), or people in general.

On ne doit pas dire cela. *(One shouldn't say that.)*

On ne sait jamais. *(You just never know.)*

On ne fait plus attention. *(People don't pay attention anymore.)*

On va partir à midi. *(We're going to leave at noon.)*

Ils versus elles

Ils and elles mean *they.* Ils refers to more than one male (or masculine noun) or to a combined group of males and females (or masculine and feminine nouns), no matter the number of each gender present. Elles refers to a group of females only.

Paul et David (ils) habitent à Bruxelles. *(Paul and David [they] live in Brussels.)*

Je vois mes gants. Ils sont dans ta chambre. *(I see my gloves. They're in your room.)*

Lise et Robert (ils) partent ensemble. *(Lise and Robert [they] are leaving together.)*

Ma mère et ma sœur (elles) aiment danser. *(My mother and sister [they] like to dance.)*

Je vois tes clés. Elles sont sur mon bureau. *(I see your keys. They're on my desk.)*

Conveying Thoughts in the Present Tense

You use the present tense to indicate what a subject is doing or does customarily. It can also indicate a state of being.

Nous regardons la télévision après le dîner. *(We watch television after dinner.)*

Il chante. *(He is singing.)*

The helping verbs *am, is,* and *are* aren't used in French, so be careful not to include them in your French.

Je danse. *(I am dancing.)*

In French, you can also use the present tense to ask for instructions, to make a proposal, or to discuss an action that will take place in the future.

> **Je fais le lit?** *(Shall I make the bed?)*
>
> **Je te vois demain.** *(I'll see you tomorrow.)*

You also use the present tense with the expression **depuis** + **an expression of time** to show that an action started in the past and is continuing into the present. The question is expressed as: **Depuis combien de temps...?** + present tense or **Depuis quand**...? + present tense.

> **Depuis combien de temps étudies-tu le français?** *(How long have you been studying French?)*
>
> **Depuis quand étudies-tu le français?** *(Since when have you been studying French?)*
>
> **J'étudie le français depuis deux ans.** *(I've been studying French for two years.)*

You can also use the present tense with **Il y a** + expression of time + **que** + the present tense to show that an action started in the past and is continuing into the present. The question is expressed as: **Combien de temps y a-t-il** + **que** + present tense.

> **Combien de temps y a-t-il que tu étudies le français?** *(How long have you been studying French?)*
>
> **Il y a deux ans que j'étudie le français.** *(I've been studying French for two years.)*

Communicating with regular verbs

Regular verbs are groups of verbs that are all conjugated the same way, so when you know how to conjugate one, you can conjugate them all — kind of a package deal. Verbs that aren't conjugated are in their infinitive form (the one you find in the dictionary), and the three groups of regular verbs are classified by their infinitive endings: **-er, -ir,** and **-re.** This section shows you how to get them in shape.

The present tense in French has three different meanings in English. For example, **je parle** means not only *I speak* but also *I am speaking* and *I do speak.*

Here's how it works: Take the infinitive and drop its ending (**-er, -ir,** or **-re**) and then add the endings for the subject pronouns as indicated in Table 3-2.

Table 3-2   Regular Verb Conjugation in the Present

Subject	-er Verbs	-ir Verbs	-re Verbs
	parler *(to speak)*	**finir** *(to finish)*	**vendre** *(to sell)*
je	parl**e**	fin**is**	vend**s**
tu	parl**es**	fin**is**	vend**s**
il, elle, on	parl**e**	fin**it**	vend
nous	parl**ons**	fin**issons**	vend**ons**
vous	parl**ez**	fin**issez**	vend**ez**
ils, elles	parl**ent**	fin**issent**	vend**ent**

Here are some examples of regular verbs in the present tense:

> **Tu parles français?** *(Do you speak French?)*
>
> **Elle finit ses devoirs.** *(She is finishing her homework.)*
>
> **Les Robert vendent leur voiture.** *(The Roberts are selling their car.)*

The patterns in the table above apply to all regular verbs. Next we list some common regular verbs that you may encounter in everyday life.

First up are common regular **–er** verbs:

- **adorer** *(to adore)*
- **aider** *(to help)*
- **aimer** *(to like, to love)*
- **arriver** *(to arrive)*
- **chanter** *(to sing)*
- **chercher** *(to look for)*
- **danser** *(to dance)*
- **demander** *(to ask)*
- **donner** *(to give)*

- ✔ **écouter** *(to listen to)*
- ✔ **enseigner** *(to teach)*
- ✔ **étudier** *(to study)*
- ✔ **gagner** *(to win)*
- ✔ **habiter** *(to live [somewhere])*
- ✔ **jouer** *(to play)*
- ✔ **marcher** *(to walk)*

- ✔ **penser** *(to think)*
- ✔ **porter** *(to wear, to carry)*
- ✔ **regarder** *(to watch/look at)*
- ✔ **rencontrer** *(to meet)*
- ✔ **téléphoner** *(to call)*
- ✔ **tomber** *(to fall)*
- ✔ **travailler** *(to work)*
- ✔ **trouver** *(to find)*
- ✔ **visiter** *(to visit [a place, not people])*

Next are common regular –ir verbs:

- ✔ **applaudir** *(to applaud)*
- ✔ **bâtir** *(to build)*
- ✔ **choisir** *(to choose)*
- ✔ **établir** *(to establish)*
- ✔ **finir** *(to finish)*
- ✔ **grandir** *(to grow [up])*
- ✔ **grossir** *(to gain weight)*

- ✔ **maigrir** *(to lose weight)*
- ✔ **obéir (à)** *(to obey)*
- ✔ **punir** *(to punish)*
- ✔ **réagir** *(to react)*
- ✔ **réfléchir (à)** *(to reflect, to think [about])*
- ✔ **remplir** *(to fill)*
- ✔ **réunir** *(to unite, to gather, to assemble, to meet)*
- ✔ **réussir (à)** *(to succeed [in])*

Here are examples of common regular -re verbs:

- ✔ **attendre** *(to wait for)*
- ✔ **descendre** *(to go down)*
- ✔ **entendre** *(to hear)*

- ✔ **perdre** *(to lose, to waste)*
- ✔ **rendre** *(to give back, to return)*
- ✔ **répondre (à)** *(to answer)*

Changing certain verb spellings

Some verbs have the same endings as regular **-er** verbs, but for pronunciation reasons, they have a slight spelling change in certain conjugations. This section helps you conjugate them.

Working with -cer verbs

In French, the letter **c** has two sounds: hard, like the *c* in coal, and soft, like the *c* in celery. The French **c** is:

- ✔ Hard when it precedes the vowels *a, o,* or *u.*
- ✔ Soft when it precedes *e, i,* or *y.*

The **c** at the end of **-cer** verbs is soft because it precedes **e**, which means it should be kept soft in all conjugated forms. To ensure that it remains soft, the **c** changes to **ç** before **a, o,** or **u.** Take a look at the verb table below:

prononcer (to pronounce)	
je **prononce**	nous **prononçons**
tu **prononces**	vous **prononcez**
il/elle/on **prononce**	ils/elles **prononcent**

Nous prononçons bien le français. *(We pronounce French well.)*

French has dozens of **-cer** verbs, including the following:

- ✔ **annoncer** *(to announce)*
- ✔ **avancer** *(to advance)*
- ✔ **commencer** *(to begin)*
- ✔ **effacer** *(to erase)*
- ✔ **influencer** *(to sway, influence)*
- ✔ **lancer** *(to throw)*

Managing -ger verbs

The letter **g** also has two sounds in French: hard, like the *g* in glass, and soft, like the *g* in massage. The French **g** is:

✔ Hard when it precedes *a, o,* or *u.*

✔ Soft when it precedes *e, i,* or *y.*

The **g** at the end of **-ger** verbs is soft, so it should be kept soft in all its conjugated forms. To avoid the hard **g** in the present-tense **nous** form of the verb, you add an **e.** See the table below for an example:

bouger (to move)	
je **bouge**	nous **bougeons**
tu **bouges**	vous **bougez**
il/elle/on **bouge**	ils/elles **bougent**

> **Je ne** bouge pas de chez moi ce soir. *(I'm staying at home tonight [not moving from my house].)*

French has dozens of **-ger** verbs, including these:

✔ **arranger** *(to arrange)*

✔ **changer** *(to change)*

✔ **corriger** *(to correct)*

✔ **déménager** *(to move [from one's house])*

✔ **déranger** *(to disturb)*

✔ **diriger** *(to direct)*

✔ **exiger** *(to demand, insist)*

✔ **manger** *(to eat)*

✔ **nager** *(to swim)*

✔ **partager** *(to share)*

✔ **voyager** *(to travel)*

Tackling -yer verbs

Verbs that end in **-yer** have two stems:

✔ A regular stem with **y** for the **nous** and **vous** conjugations.

✔ An irregular stem with **i** in place of **y** for the other conjugations.

This stem change is required for verbs that end in **-oyer** and **-uyer**. Here we conjugate **employer** *(to employ)*.

employer (to employ, make use of)	
j'**emploie**	nous **employons**
tu **emploies**	vous **employez**
il/elle/on **emploie**	ils/elles **emploient**

> **Tu emploies bien ton temps.** *(You make good use of your time.)*

There are dozens of **-yer** verbs, such as

- ✔ **ennuyer** *(to bore, annoy)*
- ✔ **envoyer** *(to send)*
- ✔ **essuyer** *(to wipe)*
- ✔ **nettoyer** *(to clean)*
- ✔ **tutoyer** *(to address someone using **tu**)*
- ✔ **vouvoyer** *(to address someone using **vous**)*

This change is optional for verbs that end in **-ayer**, like **payer** *(to pay)*. **Je paie** and **je paye** are both acceptable. Similar verbs are **effrayer** *(to frighten)* and **essayer** *(to try)*.

Figuring out -eler verbs

Verbs that end in **-eler** have a regular stem with a single **l** in the nous and vous conjugations and an irregular **ll** for the other conjugations. This example shows the conjugation for **épeler** *(to spell)*.

épeler (to spell)	
j'**épelle**	nous **épelons**
tu **épelles**	vous **épelez**
il/elle/on **épelle**	ils/elles **épellent**

> **Vous épelez bien.** *(You spell well.)*

There are only a few **-eler** verbs:

- ✔ **appeler** *(to call)*
- ✔ **rappeler** *(to call back, recall)*
- ✔ **renouveler** *(to renew)*

The verbs **geler** *(to freeze)* and **peler** *(to peel)* don't follow this pattern of doubling the **l.** You conjugate them like **-e*er** verbs. (See the "Looking at -e*er verbs" section later in this chapter for more info.)

Focusing on -eter verbs

Some verbs that end in **-eter** have a regular stem with a single **t** in the present-tense **nous** and **vous** conjugations and an irregular **tt** for the other conjugations. See how you conjugate **jeter** *(to throw)*.

jeter (to throw)	
je **jette**	nous **jetons**
tu **jettes**	vous **jetez**
il/elle/on **jette**	ils/elles **jettent**

Elle jette Marc à l'eau. *(She's throwing Marc in the water.)*

The most common **-eter** verbs are

- ✔ **feuilleter** *(to leaf through)*
- ✔ **projeter** *(to project)*
- ✔ **rejeter** *(to reject)*

The verb **acheter** *(to buy)* is an exception; it's conjugated like **-e*er verbs,** which we discuss next.

Looking at -e*er verbs

Verbs that end in **-e*er** have an unstressed **e** + a consonant in the syllable before the infinitive ending. Conjugated, these verbs have a regular present-tense stem with an unaccented **e** (for **nous** and **vous**) and an irregular stem with an **è** (for all other subject pronouns). Consider the following example.

mener (to lead)	
je **mène**	nous **menons**
tu **mènes**	vous **menez**
il/elle/on **mène**	ils/elles **mènent**

Il mène son enfant à l'école. *(He's taking his child to the doctor.)*

The French language has many common **-e*er** verbs (including the exceptions to the **-eler** and **-eter** verbs we mention previously in this chapter). Some of these verbs include the following:

- ✔ **acheter** *(to buy)*
- ✔ **amener** *(to bring [along])*
- ✔ **élever** *(to bring up, raise)*
- ✔ **emmener** *(to take away)*
- ✔ **enlever** *(to remove)*
- ✔ **geler** *(to freeze)*
- ✔ **lever** *(to lift, raise)*
- ✔ **peser** *(to weigh)*
- ✔ **promener** *(to walk)*

Dealing with -é*er verbs

Verbs that end in **-é*er** have a regular stem that keeps the acute accent **é** for present-tense **nous** and **vous** and an irregular stem that changes to the **è.** The following example shows the conjugation for **gérer** *(to manage).*

gérer (to manage)	
je **gère**	nous **gérons**
tu **gères**	vous **gérez**
il/elle/on **gère**	ils/elles **gèrent**

Nous gérons le projet. *(We're managing the project.)*

Some **-é*er** verbs include:

- ✔ **célébrer** *(to celebrate)*
- ✔ **compléter** *(to complete)*
- ✔ **considérer** *(to consider)*
- ✔ **espérer** *(to hope)*
- ✔ **posséder** *(to possess)*
- ✔ **préférer** *(to prefer)*
- ✔ **répéter** *(to repeat)*
- ✔ **suggérer** *(to suggest)*
- ✔ **tolérer** *(to tolerate)*

Recognizing irregular verbs

As if all the different regular verb patterns weren't enough to remember, French also has numerous irregular verbs, which have either unique conjugations or patterns limited to just a few verbs. You just have to memorize these conjugations until they feel natural.

aller *(to go):* **je vais, tu vas, il/elle/on va, nous allons, vous allez, ils/elles vont**

avoir *(to have):* **j'ai, tu as, il/elle/on a, nous avons, vous avez, ils/elles ont**

boire *(to drink):* **je bois, tu bois, il/elle/on boit, nous buvons, vous buvez, ils/elles boivent**

conduire *(to drive):* **je conduis, tu conduis, il/elle/on conduit, nous conduisons, vous conduisez, ils/elles conduisent**

connaître *(to know):* **je connais, tu connais, il/elle/on connaît, nous connaissons, vous connaissez, ils/elles connaissent**

courir *(to run):* **je cours, tu cours, il/elle/on court, nous courons, vous courez, ils/elles courent**

croire *(to believe):* **je crois, tu crois, il/elle/on croit, nous croyons, vous croyez, ils/elles croient**

devoir *(to have to, must):* je dois, tu dois, il/elle/on doit, nous devons, vous devez, ils/elles doivent

dire *(to say, tell):* je dis, tu dis, il/elle/on dit, nous disons, vous dites, ils/elles disent

dormir *(to sleep):* je dors, tu dors, il/elle/on dort, nous dormons, vous dormez, ils/elles dorment

écrire *(to write):* j'écris, tu écris, il/elle/on écrit, nous écrivons, vous écrivez, ils/elles écrivent

être *(to be):* je suis, tu es, il/elle/on est, nous sommes, vous êtes, ils/elles sont

faire *(to make, do):* je fais, tu fais, il/elle/on fait, nous faisons, vous faites, ils/elles font

lire *(to read):* je lis, tu lis, il/elle/on lit, nous lisons, vous lisez, ils/elles lisent

mettre *(to put [on]):* je mets, tu mets, il/elle/on met, nous mettons, vous mettez, ils/elles mettent

Note that other verbs conjugated like **mettre** include **admettre** *(to admit),* **transmettre** *(to transmit),* **permettre** *(to allow),* **promettre** *(to promise),* and **remettre** *(to put back; to deliver).*

offrir *(to offer):* j'offre, tu offres, il/elle/on offre, nous offrons, vous offrez, ils/elles offrent

ouvrir *(to open):* j'ouvre, tu ouvres, il/elle/on ouvre, nous ouvrons, vous ouvrez, ils/elles ouvrent

Other verbs conjugated like **ouvrir** include **couvrir** *(to cover),* **découvrir** *(to discover),* and **souffrir** *(to suffer).*

partir *(to leave):* je pars, tu pars, il/elle/on part, nous partons, vous partez, ils/elles partent

pouvoir *(to be able to, can):* je peux, tu peux, il/elle/on peut, nous pouvons, vous pouvez, ils/elles peuvent

prendre *(to take):* je prends, tu prends, il/elle/on prend, nous prenons, vous prenez, ils/elles prennent

Other verbs conjugated like **prendre** include **apprendre** *(to learn),* **comprendre** *(to understand),* and **surprendre** *(to surprise).*

recevoir *(to receive):* **je reçois, tu reçois, il/elle/on reçoit, nous recevons, vous recevez, ils/elles reçoivent**

rire *(to laugh):* **je ris, tu ris, il/elle/on rit, nous rions, vous riez, ils/elles rient**

Another verb like **rire** is **sourire** *(to smile).*

savoir *(to know [how or facts]):* **je sais, tu sais, il/elle/on sait, nous savons, vous savez, ils/elles savent**

sentir *(to feel, smell):* **je sens, tu sens, il/elle/on sent, nous sentons, vous sentez, ils/elles sentent**

Another verb like **sentir** is **mentir** *(to lie).*

sortir *(to go out):* **je sors, tu sors, il/elle/on sort, nous sortons, vous sortez, ils/elles sortent**

suivre *(to follow):* **je suis, tu suis, il/elle/on suit, nous suivons, vous suivez, ils/elles suivent**

Another verb like **suivre** is **poursuivre** *(to pursue).*

venir *(to come):* **je viens, tu viens, il/elle/on vient, nous venons, vous venez, ils/elles viennent**

Other verbs conjugated like **venir** include: **contenir** *(to contain),* **devenir** *(to become),* **maintenir** *(to maintain),* **tenir** *(to hold),* and **revenir** *(to come back).*

vivre *(to live):* **je vis, tu vis, il/elle/on vit, nous vivons, vous vivez, ils/elles vivent**

Another verb like **vivre** is **survivre** *(to survive).*

voir *(to see):* **je vois, tu vois, il/elle/on voit, nous voyons, vous voyez, ils/elles voient**

vouloir *(to want):* **je veux, tu veux, il/elle/on veut, nous voulons, vous voulez, ils/elles veulent**

Expressing yourself with irregular verbs

The irregular verbs **aller** *(to go)*, **avoir** *(to have)*, **être** *(to be)*, and **faire** *(to make, do)* are commonly used in everyday French as part of idiomatic expressions.

High-frequency expressions that include **aller** are:

aller + adverb *(to feel, to be; describing a state of health)*	**Comment allez-vous?** *(How are you?)* **Je vais bien.** *(I'm fine.)*
aller + infinitive (to express the near future)	**Ils vont étudier.** *(They are going to study.)*

High-frequency expressions that include **avoir** are:

avoir...ans *(to be...years old)*	**Quel âge as –tu?** *(How old are you?)* **J'ai vingt ans.** *(I'm 20 years old.)*
avoir besoin de *(to need)*	**J'ai besoin d'un couteau.** *(I need a knife.)*
avoir de la chance *(to be lucky)*	**Tu as de la chance!** *(You are lucky!)*
avoir chaud (froid, faim, soif, honte [de], peur [de], raison, tort *(to be hot [person], cold [person], hungry, thirsty, ashamed [of], afraid [of], right, wrong)*	**J'ai chaud (froid, faim, soif, honte, peur, raison, tort).** *(I'm hot [cold, hungry, thirsty, ashamed, afraid, right, wrong].)*
avoir envie de *(to feel like)*	**J'ai envie de danser.** *(I feel like dancing.)*
avoir lieu *(to take place)*	**La fête a lieu à huit heures.** *(The party is taking place at 8:00 o'clock.)*
avoir mal à + body part *(to have an ache)*	**Il a mal à la tête.** *(He has a headache.)*
avoir sommeil *(to be sleepy)*	**J'ai sommeil.** *(I'm tired).*

avoir l'occasion de *(to have the opportunity to)*

As-tu l'occasion de voyager? *(Do you have the opportunity to travel?)*

avoir l'habitude de *(to be in the habit of, to be accustomed to)*

Il a l'habitude de dormir jusqu'à midi. *(He's in the habit of sleeping until noon.)*

High-frequency expressions that include **être** are:

être à *(to belong to)*

Ce livre est à moi. *(This book belongs to me.)*

être en train de *(to be in the middle [of an action])*

Ils sont en train de manger. *(They are in the middle of eating.)*

High-frequency expressions that include **faire** are:

faire + weather condition

Quel temps fait-il? *(What's the weather?)* **Il fait bon (beau, mauvais, froid, chaud, frais, lourd, du vent, du soleil).** *(It is good [beautiful, bad, cold, hot, cool, humid, windy, sunny].)*

faire + sport *(to play or engage in a sport)*

Je fais du tennis. *(I play tennis.)*

faire attention (à) *(to pay attention to)*

Je fais attention au professeur. *(I pay attention to the teacher.)*

faire la connaissance de *(to make someone's acquaintance, meet)*

Il a fait la connaissance de mon frère. *(He met my brother.)*

faire la queue *(to form a line)*

On fait la queue devant le cinéma. *(They are making a line in front of the movies.)*

faire un voyage *(to take a trip)*

Faites-vous un voyage en France? *(Are you taking a trip to France?)*

faire une promenade *(to take a walk)*

Nous faisons une promenade le soir. *(We take a walk at night.)*

Identifying reflexive verbs

Reflexive verbs tell you that someone is doing something to himself or herself. Whenever you look at yourself in the mirror or buy yourself something at the mall, you're involved in a reflexive action. In English, reflexive actions become a little tricky because so much is considered as understood. French, however, requires the use of a reflexive verb to show a reflexive action.

Every reflexive verb has a reflexive pronoun in front of it. The addition of the reflexive pronoun doesn't necessarily change the meaning of the verb, but it alerts you that the subject is performing the action on itself. You can recognize a reflexive verb by the reflexive pronoun **se** that precedes the infinitive: **se coucher** *(to go to bed)*, **se laver** *(to wash oneself)*, and so on.

You can use most reflexive verbs without the reflexive pronoun, but then the meaning changes: Alone, **laver** means *to wash (someone/something else).* Used reflexively, it means *to wash oneself or a part of oneself.* For example:

> **Je lave la voiture.** *(I am washing the car.)*
>
> **Je me lave.** *(I am washing myself.)*
>
> **Je me lave les mains.** *(I am washing my hands.)*

When you use a part of the body with a reflexive verb, you use the definite article before the part of the body, not the possessive adjective.

> **Je me lave la figure.** *(I wash my face.)*

Table 3-3 shows reflexive verbs and the reflexive pronoun for each subject.

Table 3-3	Properly Using Reflexive Pronouns		
Infinitive	*Subject*	*Reflexive Pronoun*	*Verb*
se laver *(to wash oneself)*	je	me	lave
se lever *(to get up)*	tu	te	lèves
se raser *(to shave)*	il, elle, on	se	rase

Infinitive	Subject	Reflexive Pronoun	Verb
se coucher *(to go to bed)*	**nous**	**nous**	**couchons**
se reposer *(to rest)*	**vous**	**vous**	**reposez**
se promener *(to go for a walk)*	**ils, elles**	**se**	**promènent**

The reflexive pronoun **se** becomes **s'** before a vowel or a mute h.

Ella s'amuse. *(She has fun.)*

Il s'inquiète. *(He worries.)*

Don't forget to make all necessary spelling changes:

Je me lève. *(I get up.)*

The verbs in this list can be reflexive or non-reflexive:

- ✔ **s'appeler** *(to call oneself, to be named)*
- ✔ **s'arrêter** *(to stop oneself)*
- ✔ **s'habiller** *(to dress oneself, to get dressed)*
- ✔ **se baigner** *(to bathe oneself)*
- ✔ **se brosser** *(to brush)*
- ✔ **se coiffer** *(to do/style one's hair)*
- ✔ **se coucher** *(to go to bed, to put oneself to bed)*
- ✔ **se couper** *(to cut oneself)*
- ✔ **se laver** *(to wash oneself)*
- ✔ **se lever** *(to get up, to get oneself up)*
- ✔ **se maquiller** *(to put makeup on oneself)*
- ✔ **se peigner** *(to comb one's hair)*
- ✔ **se promener** *(to take oneself for a walk, to stroll)*
- ✔ **se raser** *(to shave oneself)*
- ✔ **se réveiller** *(to wake oneself up)*

Reciprocal verbs convey a reciprocal action between two subjects or more. The subject pronoun **on** can often refer to a plural subject pronoun like *we* or *they*. Check out the following examples:

> **On s'écrit tous les jours.** *(We write to each other every day.)*

> **Ils se voient souvent.** *(They see each other often.)*

Even when **on** has a plural meaning, you always conjugate the verb in the third-person singular.

The following list shows the common verbs that may show reciprocal action.

- ✔ **s'aimer** *(to love each other)*
- ✔ **s'écrire** *(to write to each other)*
- ✔ **s'embrasser** *(to kiss each other)*
- ✔ **se comprendre** *(to understand each other)*
- ✔ **se connaître** *(to know each other)*
- ✔ **se disputer** *(to argue with each other)*
- ✔ **se parler** *(to speak to each other)*
- ✔ **se promettre** *(to promise each other)*
- ✔ **se quitter** *(to leave each other)*
- ✔ **se regarder** *(to look at each other)*
- ✔ **se rencontrer** *(to meet each other)*
- ✔ **se retrouver** *(to find each other)*
- ✔ **se téléphoner** *(to call each other)*
- ✔ **se voir** *(to see each other)*

Finally, there are verbs that have one meaning when they are not reflexive and a different meaning when they are reflexive, as shown in Table 3-4.

Table 3-4	Different Verb Meanings		
Usual Verb	**Translation**	**Idiomatic Verb**	**Translation**
amuser	to amuse, to entertain	**s'amuser**	to have fun
débrouiller	to disentangle	**se débrouiller**	to manage
demander	to ask	**se demander**	to wonder
dépêcher	to dispatch	**se dépêcher**	to hurry, to be in a hurry
douter	to doubt	**se douter de**	to suspect
ennuyer	to bother	**s'ennuyer**	to be bored
inquiéter	to disturb someone	**s'inquiéter**	to become worried
mettre	to put, to place	**se mettre à**	to begin (to do something)
occuper	to occupy, to hold	**s'occuper de**	to be in charge of, to take care of, to deal with
passer	to pass	**se passer**	to happen
rappeler	to call back	**se rappeler**	to remember, to recall
servir	to serve	**se servir de**	to use
tromper	to deceive, to disappoint	**se tromper de**	to be mistaken, to be wrong

Just as with direct and indirect object pronouns (refer to Chapter 2), you generally place reflexive pronouns before the conjugated verbs.

> **Elle se dépêche.** *(She is hurrying.)*

When you have a conjugated verb followed by an infinitive, the reflexive pronoun goes in front of the infinitive.

> **Nous allons nous acheter de la glace.** *(We're going to buy ourselves some ice cream.)*

Negatives are placed around the conjugated verb. (See Chapter 6 for more about negation.)

> **Elle ne va pas se maquiller.** *(She's not going to put on makeup.)*

The only times you don't put the reflexive pronoun right in front of the reflexive verb are in the following situations:

- ✔ **Affirmative imperative:** In affirmative commands, you place the reflexive pronoun after the verb and connect the two words with hyphens. Note that **te** changes to **toi**. (See Chapter 9.)

  Lève-toi. *(Get up.)*

  Dépêchez-vous. *(Hurry up.)*

- ✔ **Compound tenses:** In the passé composé the reflexive pronoun precedes the helping verb **être.** (See Chapter 7.)

  Je me suis levé très tôt. *(I got up very early.)*

  Vous vous êtes trompés. *(You made a mistake.)*

- ✔ **Questions with inversion:** When you use inversion to ask questions with reflexive verbs, the reflexive pronoun precedes the inverted verb-subject (See Chapter 6.)

  Te douches-tu le matin ou le soir? *(Do you shower in the morning or at night?)*

  Vous êtes-vous levés avant 7h00? *(Did you get up before 7 a.m.?)*

Understanding Present Participles and Gerunds

In English, the present participle is a verb form that ends in *–ing.* A gerund looks like a verb but actually works as a noun.

Forming the present participle

In English, the present participle always ends in *-ing:* singing, walking, and so on. In French, the present participle ends in **–ant: chantant** *(singing)* and **marchant** *(walking).*

Forming the present participle is easy for regular verbs and for most irregular verbs. Simply take the **nous** form of any present-tense verb, drop the **-ons** ending, and add **-ant.** Table 3-5 shows the present participle for some regular, irregular, and spelling change verbs.

Table 3-5	Forming the Present Participle	
Infinitive	*Nous Form*	*Present Participle*
aller	allons	allant *(going)*
appeler	appelons	appelant *(calling)*
commencer	commençons	commençant *(beginning)*
faire	faisons	faisant *(doing)*
finir	finissons	finissant *(finishing)*
manger	mangeons	mangeant *(eating)*
parler	parlons	parlant *(speaking)*
partir	partons	partant *(leaving)*
préférer	préférons	préférant *(preferring)*
prendre	prenons	prenant *(taking)*
vendre	vendons	vendant *(selling)*
venir	venons	venant *(coming)*
voir	voyons	voyant *(seeing)*

Only three verbs have an irregular present participle. They are:

✓ **avoir** *(to have):* **ayant** *(having)*

✓ **être** *(to be):* **étant** *(being)*

✓ **savoir** *(to know):* **sachant** *(knowing)*

Using the present participle

You can use the present participle as follows:

- ✔ To indicate cause or circumstances:

  Ayant de l'argent, elle a pu voyager. *(Having some money, she was able to travel.)*
- ✔ As an adjective:

  C'est une histoire intéressante. *(It's an interesting story.)*
- ✔ As a noun:

  Ils regardent les passants. *(They are watching the passersby.)*

Using gerunds

A gerund in French is the past participle preceded by **en,** which means *while, as,* or *by* in English. Because the gerund modifies another verb, it's essentially acting as an adverb. To use the present participle as a gerund, just put **en** in front of it and any descriptive information after.

> **La fille chante en marchant.** *(The girl is singing while walking.)*

> **J'écoute la radio en travaillant.** *(I listen to the radio while working.)*

You can also use the gerund to express manner or circumstances.

> **En entrant dans le bâtiment, j'ai vu Paul.** *(Upon entering the building, I saw Paul.)*

> **J'ai compris la situation en lisant les journaux.** *(I understood the situation upon/in/by reading the newspapers.)*

A French present participle, unlike an English gerund (an *-ing* verb acting as a noun), may not be used as a noun subject or after a conjugated verb.

> **La natation est mon sport préféré.** *(Swimming is my favorite sport.)*

> **Je préfère rester à la maison.** *(I prefer staying [to stay] at home.)*

Chapter 4

Being Descriptive and Connecting Your Thoughts

In This Chapter

▶ Understanding adjectives

▶ Using adverbs correctly

▶ Making comparisons

*W*hile nouns and verbs are the building blocks and actions of language, adjectives and adverbs are the colors, shapes, sizes, speeds, frequencies, and styles that bring those blocks and actions to life. So adjectives and adverbs provide detail and clarification to the nouns, verbs, and other words they modify. This chapter explains all about adjectives and adverbs, including how to use them, where to put them in the sentence, the different types, and how to make comparisons.

Coloring with Adjectives

Adjectives describe nouns and pronouns. Is the house *big*? Are the trees *green*? You can use adjectives so that people will have the most information about, and the best possible understanding of, what you want to describe. This section focuses on what you need to know about adjectives.

Making adjectives agree

In French, adjectives have to agree with a noun or pronoun in gender and number. Most of the rules for making adjectives feminine and plural are the same as those for making nouns feminine and plural (see Chapter 2).

The masculine singular is the default form of the adjective — that's what you'd look up in the dictionary. Your dictionary likely doesn't have entries for the feminine equivalents or plurals, except when they are irregular.

The gender of adjectives

In order to make a masculine adjective feminine, all you have to do for many adjectives is add an **-e** to the end of the masculine singular form. If the masculine adjective already ends in silent **e,** you don't make any changes to get the feminine form.

Masculine	*Feminine*
petit *(small)*	**petite**
joli *(pretty)*	**jolie**
préféré *(favorite)*	**préférée**
bleu *(blue)*	**bleue**
grave *(serious)*	**grave**
rouge *(red)*	**rouge**

For masculine adjectives that end in **–x**, change **–x** to **–se.**

Masculine	*Feminine*
curieux *(curious)*	**curieuse**
délicieux *(delicious)*	**délicieuse**
heureux *(happy)*	**heureuse**
malheureux *(unhappy)*	**malheureuse**
paresseux *(lazy)*	**paresseuse**
sérieux *(serious)*	**sérieuse**

For masculine adjectives that end in **–f,** change **-f** to **–ve:**

Masculine	*Feminine*
actif *(active)*	**active**
attentif *(attentive)*	**attentive**
naïf *(naive)*	**naïve**
sportif *(athletic)*	**sportive**
vif *(lively)*	**vive**

For masculine adjectives ending in **–er,** change **–er** to **ère.**

Masculine	*Feminine*
cher *(dear, expensive)*	**chère**
dernier *(last)*	**dernière**
entier *(entire, whole)*	**entière**
étranger *(foreign)*	**étrangère**
fier *(proud)*	**fière**
léger *(light)*	**légère**
premier *(first)*	**première**

Some masculine adjectives, double the final consonant before adding **–e.**

Masculine	*Feminine*
ancien *(old, former, ancient)*	**ancienne**
bas *(low)*	**basse**
bon *(good)*	**bonne**
cruel *(cruel)*	**cruelle**
européen *(European)*	**européenne**
formel *(formal)*	**formelle**
gentil *(nice)*	**gentille**
gros *(fat)*	**grosse**
intellectuel *(intellectual)*	**intellectuelle**
italien *(Italian)*	**italienne**
mignon *(cute)*	**mignonne**
pareil *(similar)*	**pareille**
tel *(such)*	**telle**

Adjectives that refer to nationalities and religions aren't capitalized in French.

> **J'ai une correspondante française.** *(I have a French penpal.)*

French also has several other irregular feminine forms. The most common are shown in the following table.

Masculine	Feminine	English
blanc	blanche	white
complet	complète	complete
doux	douce	sweet, soft, mild, gentle
faux	fausse	false
favori	favorite	favorite
frais	fraîche	fresh, cool
franc	franche	frank
inquiet	inquiète	worried, uneasy
long	longue	long
public	publique	public
sec	sèche	dry
secret	secrète	secret
travailleur	travailleuse	hardworking, industrious

Some French adjectives have an extra form that precedes a masculine singular noun or a masculine singular adjective that begins with a vowel or mute h. Its goal is to make pronunciation easier so you don't have to say back-to-back vowel sounds. See Table 4-1.

Table 4-1 Adjectives with Special Masculine Singular Forms

English	Masc. Singular	Masc. Singular before a Vowel or Mute h	Fem. Singular	Masc. Plural	Fem. Plural
beautiful	beau	bel	belle	beaux	belles
new	nouveau	nouvel	nouvelle	nouveaux	nouvelles
crazy	fou	fol	folle	fous	folles
soft	mou	mol	molle	mous	molles
old	vieux	vieil	vieille	vieux	vieilles

Here are examples:

un bel homme (*a handsome man*)

mon nouvel avocat (*my new lawyer*)

The plural of adjectives

In order to make most French adjectives plural, whether they are masculine or feminine, all you do is add an **-s.**

Singular	Plural
joli *(pretty)*	**jolis**
fatigué *(tired)*	**fatigués**
blanche *(white)*	**blanches**
bonne *(good)*	**bonnes**
actif *(active)*	**actifs**

Singular adjectives ending in **–s** or **–x** do not change in the plural.

Singular	Plural
gris *(gray)*	**gris**
heureux *(happy)*	**heureux**

Most adjectives that end in **-al** change **–al** to **–aux** in the plural.

Singular	Plural
général *(general)*	**généraux**
génial *(great)*	**géniaux**
loyal *(loyal)*	**loyaux**
original *(original)*	**originaux**
spécial *(special)*	**spéciaux**

The masculine singular adjective **tout** *(all)* is irregular and becomes **tous** in the masculine plural.

> **Tous les garçons jouent au tennis.** *(All the boys are playing tennis.)*

Pay careful attention to the following plurals.

Singular	Plural
beau (bel) *(beautiful)*	**beaux**
fou (fol) *(crazy)*	**fous**
mou (mol) *(soft)*	**mous**
nouveau (nouvel) *(new)*	**nouveaux**
vieux (vieil) *(old)*	**vieux**

Here are some examples:

>**le nouveau garage** → **les nouveaux garages**
>
>**le nouvel hotel** → **les nouveaux hôtels**

Use the masculine plural form of the adjective when speaking about nouns of different genders.

>**Ma soeur et mon frère sont blonds.** (*My sister and my brother are blond.*)
>
>**La maison et l'appartement sont beaux.** (*The house and the apartment are beautiful.*)

Positioning adjectives

In French, adjectives may precede or follow the noun they modify. Most adjectives follow the noun. The placement depends on the type of adjective being used, the connotation the speaker wants to convey, and the emphasis being used. And sometimes, when more than one adjective describes a noun, the rules for placement vary according to the type of adjectives being used. The following sections dig deeper into these topics.

Adjectives that follow the noun

Most descriptive French adjectives — that is, adjectives that describe the nature or appearance of a noun, such as color, shape, or origin — follow the nouns they modify.

>**une voiture verte** (*a green car*)
>
>**un garçon mince** (*a slender boy*)
>
>**des vêtements européens** (*European clothing*)
>
>**une fille heureuse** (*a happy girl*)

In addition, present and past participles used as adjectives always follow nouns (see Chapters 3 and 7 for more on participles).

>**des yeux étincelants** (*sparkling eyes*)
>
>**une histoire compliquée** (*a complicated story*)

Adjectives that precede the noun

A few descriptive adjectives come before nouns. Descriptive adjectives that refer to the following qualities generally come in front of the nouns they modify (you can remember them with the acronym BAGS):

✔ Beauty **(beau, joli)**

✔ Age **(nouveau, jeune, vieux)**

✔ Goodness and badness **(bon, mauvais, gentil, vilain)**

✔ Size **(court, long, gros, petit, grand)**

Here are some examples. Note that **des** becomes **de** when the adjective precedes the noun.

> **une jolie femme** *(a pretty woman)*
>
> **une nouvelle voiture** *(a new car)*
>
> **un jeune homme** *(a young man)*
>
> **une bonne idée** *(a good idea)*
>
> **de mauvaises nouvelles** *(some bad news)*
>
> **de petits appartements** *(some small apartments)*

Other common adjectives that precede the noun are:

✔ **autre** *(other)*

✔ **plusieurs** *(several)*

✔ **quelques** *(a few, some)*

✔ **chaque** *(each)*

✔ **premier** *(first)*

✔ **tel** *(such)*

✔ **dernier** *(last)*

✔ **quelque** *(some)*

✔ **tout** *(all, every)*

Here are some examples:

> **J'ai plusieurs questions.** *(I have several questions.)*
>
> **As-tu un autre stylo?** *(Do you have another pen?)*

Changing meanings

Some French adjectives have different meanings depending on whether they precede or follow the noun. When these adjectives have a literal meaning, you place them after the noun. When they have a figurative meaning, you place them before the noun.

un ancien médecin *(former doctor)*

un médecin ancien *(old doctor)*

la pauvre femme *(poor, wretched woman)*

la femme pauvre *(poor, penniless woman)*

See Table 4-2 for some common French adjectives with meaning changes.

Table 4-2   Adjectives Whose Meanings Change

Adjective	Meaning before Noun	Meaning after Noun
brave	good, decent	brave
cher	dear (cherished)	expensive
curieux	odd, strange	inquisitive
dernier	final	previous
franc	real, genuine	frank
pauvre	unfortunate	poor (without money)
premier	first	basic, primary
prochain	following	next
propre	(my, his, our) own	clean
sale	dirty (nasty)	dirty (soiled)
triste	sorry, pathetic	sad

Describing Actions with Adverbs

Different types of adverbs have different purposes, and the type you want to use depends on what you want to say — are you talking about how often something happens, where it happens, when, . . .? Adverb position depends in part on the type of adverb you're using.

Creating adverbs

Many adverbs are formed from adjectives, in both French and English. These adverbs express how something happens, and they usually end in *-ly* in English *(clearly, quickly, frankly)*, and in **-ment** in French **(clairement, rapidement, franchement).**

Adverbs of manner

The rules for turning adjectives into adverbs are fairly straightforward. For masculine adjectives that end in a single vowel, just add **–ment.**

Adjective	Meaning	Adverb	Meaning
poli	*polite*	poliment	*politely*
carré	*square*	carrément	*squarely*
triste	*sad*	tristement	*sadly*

Other words need a little more tweaking. Keep the following rules in mind when forming adverbs:

✔ When the masculine adjective ends in a consonant (except for **-ant** or **-ent**) or multiple vowels, take the feminine form of the adjective and add **-ment.**

Masc. Adj.	Fem. Adj.	Adverb	Meaning
certain	certaine	certainement	*(certainly)*
heureux	heureuse	heureusement	*(happily, fortunately)*
dernier	dernière	dernièrement	*(lastly)*
nouveau	nouvelle	nouvellement	*(newly)*

✔ For adjectives that end in **-ant** or **-ent,** replace that ending with **-amment** or **–emment.**

Masc. Adj.	Adverb	Meaning
constant	constamment	*(constantly)*
évident	évidemment	*(evidently)*
intelligent	intelligemment	*(intelligently)*
récent	récemment	*(recently)*

However, remember a few specific exceptions to the preceding rules:

- ✔ **énorme** *(enormous)* becomes **énormément** *(enormously)*
- ✔ **gentil** *(nice, kind)* becomes **gentiment** *(nicely, kindly)*
- ✔ **lent** *(slow)* becomes **lentement** *(slowly)*
- ✔ **vrai** *(true)* becomes **vraiment** *(truly)*

Some French adverbs of manner don't end in **–ment.**

- ✔ **bien** *(well)*
- ✔ **debout** *(standing up)*
- ✔ **exprès** *(on purpose)*
- ✔ **mal** *(poorly, badly)*
- ✔ **mieux** *(better)*
- ✔ **pire** *(worse)*
- ✔ **vite** *(quickly)*
- ✔ **volontiers** *(gladly)*

Here are some sentences that use adverbs of manner:

> **Elle parle très poliment.** *(She speaks very politely.)*

> **Tu l'as fait exprès!** *(You did it on purpose!)*

Adverbs of frequency

Adverbs of frequency express how often or how consistently something happens.

- ✔ **encore** *(again)*
- ✔ **jamais** *(ever)*
- ✔ **parfois** *(sometimes)*
- ✔ **quelquefois** *(sometimes)*
- ✔ **rarement** *(rarely)*
- ✔ **souvent** *(often)*
- ✔ **toujours** *(always, still)*

Check out some examples:

> **Je vais souvent aux musées.** *(I often go to museums.)*
>
> **Habites-tu toujours au Québec?** *(Do you still live in Quebec?)*

Adverbs of place

Adverbs of place tell you where something happens:

- ✔ **autour** *(around)*
- ✔ **dedans** *(inside)*
- ✔ **dehors** *(outside)*
- ✔ **derrière** *(behind, in back)*
- ✔ **dessous** *(below)*
- ✔ **dessus** *(above)*
- ✔ **devant** *(in front)*
- ✔ **en bas** *(below, down[stairs])*
- ✔ **en haut** *(up[stairs])*
- ✔ **ici** *(here)*
- ✔ **là** *(there)*
- ✔ **loin** *(far away)*
- ✔ **partout** *(everywhere)*
- ✔ **près** *(near)*
- ✔ **quelque part** *(somewhere)*

Take a look at some example sentences:

> **Je préfère m'asseoir derrière.** *(I prefer sitting in the back.)*
>
> **Qui habite en haut?** *(Who lives upstairs?)*

Many adverbs of place are also prepositions. The difference is that an adverb acts by itself to modify a verb — **J'habite en bas.** *(I live below.)* — and a preposition joins its object (the noun that follows it) with another word — **J'habite en bas de Michel.** *(I live below Michel).* See Chapter 5 for more information about French prepositions.

Adverbs of time

Adverbs of time explain when something happens.

- ✔ **actuellement** *(currently)*
- ✔ **après** *(after)*
- ✔ **aujourd'hui** *(today)*
- ✔ **aussitôt** *(immediately)*
- ✔ **autrefois** *(formerly, in the past)*
- ✔ **avant** *(before)*
- ✔ **bientôt** *(soon)*
- ✔ **d'abord** *(first, at first)*
- ✔ **déjà** *(already)*
- ✔ **demain** *(tomorrow)*
- ✔ **depuis** *(since)*
- ✔ **enfin** *(at last, finally)*
- ✔ **ensuite** *(next)*
- ✔ **hier** *(yesterday)*
- ✔ **immédiatement** *(immediately)*
- ✔ **longtemps** *(for a long time)*
- ✔ **maintenant** *(now)*
- ✔ **récemment** *(recently)*
- ✔ **tard** *(late)*
- ✔ **tôt** *(early)*

Actuellement means *currently,* not *actually.* **En fait** means *actually.*

Here are some sentences that use adverbs of time:

> **Nous allons partir demain.** *(We're going to leave tomorrow.)*
>
> **J'ai enfin visité Paris.** *(I finally visited Paris.)*

Adverbs of quantity

Adverbs of quantity tell you how many or how much of something.

- ✔ **assez (de)** *(quite, fairly, enough)*
- ✔ **autant (de)** *(as much, as many)*
- ✔ **beaucoup (de)** *(a lot, many)*
- ✔ **combien (de)** *(how many, how much)*
- ✔ **moins (de)** *(less, fewer)*
- ✔ **pas mal de** *(quite a few)*
- ✔ **(un) peu (de)** *(few, little, not very)*
- ✔ **la plupart de** *(most)*
- ✔ **plus (de)** *(more)*
- ✔ **tant (de)** *(so much, so many)*
- ✔ **très** *(very)*
- ✔ **trop (de)** *(too much, too many)*

The parentheses around **de** in many of these phrases indicate that the **de** is required only if followed by a noun. For example:

> **C'est combien?** *(How much is it?)*
>
> **Combien de voitures avez-vous?** *(How many cars do you have?)*

You can also use these adverbs of quantity as adjectives, to modify nouns.

> **Il y a trop de circulation.** *(There's too much traffic.)*
>
> **Il a beaucoup d'amis.** *(He has a lot of friends.)*

La plupart is always followed by **de** and is often followed by the third-person **(ils, elles)** verb form.

> **La plupart des gens viennent ce soir.** *(Most of the people are coming tonight.)*

but

> **La plupart du livre est intéressant.** (*Most of the book is interesting.*)

Placing adverbs

The position of French adverbs depends on what they're modifying and the type of adverb. Read on.

After the verb

When French adverbs modify a verb, they usually follow it.

> **Je le ferai volontiers!** (*I'll gladly do it!*)
>
> **Nous voyageons souvent en été.** (*We often travel in the summer.*)

If there are two verbs, the adverb goes after the conjugated verb, not after the infinitive or past participle (See Chapter 7).

> **J'aime beaucoup nager.** (*I like swimming a lot.*)
>
> **Il a déjà mangé.** (*He already ate.*)

When you negate a sentence with an adverb following a verb, the second part of the negative structure (explained in Chapter 6) comes before the adverb.

> **Je ne me sens pas bien.** (*I don't feel well.*)
>
> **Il ne travaille jamais vite.** (*He never works quickly.*)

Other places

You can put adverbs that refer to a point in time like **aujourd'hui** (*today*) and **hier** (*yesterday*) at the beginning or at the end of the sentence.

> **Je dois travailler aujourd'hui.** (*I have to work today.*)

The same is true for long adverbs.

> **Normalement, je me lève à 7h00.** (*Usually, I get up at 7 a.m.*)

When you want to stress the meaning of the adverb, you put it after the conjugated verb.

> **Il a violemment critiqué la nouvelle loi.** *(He strongly criticized the new law.)*

The best place for adverbs of place is after the direct object or, if there isn't one, after the verb.

> **Tu trouveras tes valises en haut.** *(You'll find your suitcases upstairs.)*

> **J'aimerais vivre ici.** *(I'd like to live here.)*

Adverbs that modify adjectives or other adverbs go in front of those words.

> **Elle est très belle.** *(She is very beautiful.)*

> **J'habite ici depuis assez longtemps.** *(I've lived here for a fairly long time.)*

Comparing Things

The two kinds of comparisons you can make in French are comparatives and superlatives. Comparatives say that something is more _____ than, less _____ than, or as _____ as something else; superlatives proclaim that something is the most _____ or least _____ of all.

Comparatives can indicate one of two things:

- ✔ Inequality
- ✔ Equality

Comparisons of inequality

You use **plus** *(more)* or **moins** *(less)* in French to indicate inequality with either adjectives or adverbs. **Que** *(than)* introduces the second half of the comparative construction.

Adjectives are compared as follows:

> **Positive: Elle est belle.** *(She is beautiful.)*

> **Comparative: Elle est plus (moins) belle que moi.** *(She is more [less] beautiful than I am.)*

> **Superlative: Elle est la plus (moins) belle de la classe.** *(She is the most [least] beautiful in the class.)*

Comparative and superlative forms of adjectives agree in number and gender with the nouns they modify.

> **Paul est plus grand que Camille.** *(Paul is taller than Camille.)*

> **Camille est plus grande que Paul.** *(Camille is taller than Paul.)*

Note that in the superlative the definite article must agree in number and gender with the subject.

> **Suzanne est la plus grande de la famille.** *(Susan is the tallest in the family.)*

In French comparatives, you use a stress pronoun (see Chapter 5) after **que** *(than)*. The stress pronouns are:

Singular	*Plural*
moi *(me)*	**nous** *(we)*
toi *(you)*	**vous** *(you)*
lui/elle *(he, she)*	**eux/elles** *(they)*

In French superlatives, you may use the preposition **de** + article **(du, de l', de la, des)** after the superlative to express "in" or "of."

> **La France est le plus beau pays du monde.** *(France is the most beautiful country in the world.)*

Adjectives generally retain their normal position in the superlative.

> **C'est une belle maison.** *(It's a beautiful house.)*

> **C'est la plus belle maison.** *(It's the most beautiful house.)*

When a superlative adjective follows the noun, the article is repeated.

> **Il est l'homme le plus beau.** *(He is the most handsome man.)*

but

> **Il est le plus bel homme.** *(He is the most handsome man.)*

If the object you're comparing to is implied or has already been mentioned, you can leave out the **que.**

> **J'ai lu ton livre, mais mon livre est plus intéressant.**
> *(I read your book, but my book is more interesting.)*

You can also make comparisons with two adjectives.

> **Je suis plus agacé que fâché.** *(I'm more annoyed than [I am] angry.)*

A few adjectives have irregular comparatives and superlatives.

Positive	*Comparative*	*Superlative*
bon (bons) (m) (good)	**meilleur(s)** (better)	**le (les) meilleur(s)** (best)
bonne (bonnes) (f) (good)	**meilleure(s)** (better)	**la (les) meilleure(s)** (best)
mauvais (m) (bad)	**plus mauvais** (worse)	**le (les) plus mauvais** (the worst)
mauvaise(s) (f) (bad)	**plus mauvaise(s)** (worse)	**la (les) plus mauvaise(s)** (the worst)
mauvais (m) (bad)	**pire(s)** (worse)	**le (les) pire(s)** (the worst)
mauvaise(s) (f) (bad)	**pire(s)** (worse)	**la (les) pire(s)** (the worst)

Remember that all adjectives have to agree with the nouns they modify. Here are some example sentences:

> **Ton vélo est meilleur.** *(Your bike is better.)*

> **Ma question est la meilleure.** *(My question is the best.)*

Cette décision est plus mauvaise (pire) que l'autre. *(This decision is worse than the other one.)*

Ces problèmes sont les plus mauvais (les pires). *(These problems are the worst.)*

Moins may be used with **bon** or **mauvais.**

Leurs idées sont moins bonnes. *(Their ideas are less good/aren't as good.)*

Adverbs are compared as follows:

- ✔ Positive: **Je conduis vite.** *(I drive quickly.)*

- ✔ Comparative: **Je conduis plus (moins) vite que toi.** *(I drive more [less] quickly than you.)*

- ✔ Superlative: **Je conduis le plus (moins) vite de tous mes amis.** *(I drive the most [least] quickly of all my friends.)*

The preposition **de,** or any of its forms **(du, de l', de la, des)** may follow the superlative adverb to mean "in" or "of."

De tous les ouvriers, il travaille le plus soigneusement. *(Of all the workers, he works the most carefully.)*

The article in the superlative is always **le** because there is no agreement of adjectives.

Marie parle français le plus couramment de tous les élèves. *(Marie speaks French the most fluently of all the students.)*

A few adverbs have irregular comparatives and superlatives.

Positive	*Comparative*	*Superlative*
bien *(well)*	**mieux** *(better)*	**le mieux** *([the] best)*
mal *(badly)*	**plus mal** *(worse)* / **pis** *(worse)*	**le plus mal** *([the] worst)* / **le pis** *([the] worst)*
beaucoup *(much)*	**plus** *(more)*	**le plus** *([the] most)*
peu *(little)*	**moins** *(less)*	**le moins** *([the] least)*

Here are some examples:

Elle chante mieux que lui. *(She sings better than he does.)*

Je me sens le plus mal. *(I feel [the] worst.)*

(Le) plus mal and **le pire** are preferred to **(le) pis.**

Il joue du piano le pire de tous. *(He plays the piano the worst of everyone.)*

Comparisons of equality

You express equality with **aussi** + adjective or adverb + **que** in French. This is equivalent to *as . . . as* in English.

L'exercice est aussi important que la nutrition. *(Exercise is as important as nutrition.)*

Tu t'exerces aussi consciencieusement que moi. *(You train as conscientiously as I do.)*

Chapter 5

Connecting with Prepositions

In This Chapter

▶ Putting common prepositions to work

▶ Employing prepositional pronouns

▶ Joining prepositions with places

▶ Recognizing verbs that require prepositions

*P*repositions are words that join different words, clauses, or phrases and relate elements in a sentence. In this chapter, we introduce you to common French prepositions and explain how to select the appropriate preposition for your sentences.

Committing Common Prepositions to Memory

Knowing how to use prepositions is not a simple matter of translation. You have to understand not only what prepositions mean but also how you use them in French. First, here's a list of the most common prepositions:

✔ **à** *(to, at, in)*

✔ **après** *(after)*

✔ **avant** *(before)*

✔ **avec** *(with)*

✔ **chez** *(at/to the home/office of)*

✔ **contre** *(against)*

✔ **dans** *(in)*

✔ **de** *(of, from, by, about)*

✔ **depuis** *(since, for)*

✔ **derrière** *(behind)*

✔ **devant** *(in front of)*

✔ **en** *(in, to)*

✔ **entre** *(between, among)*

✔ **par** *(by, through)*

✔ **parmi** *(among)*

✔ **pendant** *(during)*

✔ **pour** *(for)*

✔ **sans** *(without)*

✔ **sauf** *(except)*

✔ **selon** *(according to)*

✔ **sous** *(under)*

✔ **sur** *(on)*

✔ **vers** *(toward)*

The prepositions **à** and **de** contract with the definite articles **le** and **les** to form **au, aux,** and **du, des,** respectively.

Il va au bureau. *(He is going to the office.)*

Nous parlons des règles. *(We speak about the rules.)*

Recognizing the Prepositional Pronouns

You use stress pronouns after prepositions to refer to people, as the following table shows.

Singular	Plural
moi *(me)*	**nous** *(us)*
toi *(you)*	**vous** *(you)*
lui/elle *(him/her)*	**eux/elles** *(them)*

Je pense à lui. *(I'm thinking about him.)*

Ils marchent vers moi. *(They're walking toward me.)*

Using Prepositions with Places

In French, you use different prepositions with different places. This section clarifies the rules so you can figure out which preposition to use the next time you're traveling or talking about a specific place.

Expressing "to" or "in" a place

The prepositions **à, au, aux,** and **en** are used to express *to* or *in* before the names of places as follows:

> ✔ **en:** Use with feminine countries **(en France)**, feminine continents **(en Europe)**, feminine provinces **(en Lorraine)**, feminine islands **(en Sicile)**, or masculine countries beginning with a vowel **(en Israël).**
>
> ✔ **au (à + le):** Use with masculine countries beginning with a consonant **(au Mexique).**
>
> ✔ **aux (à + les):** Use with plural countries **(aux États-Unis).**
>
> ✔ **à:** Use with cities **(à Paris).**
>
> **Je vais en Italie.** *(I'm going to Italy.)*
>
> **Ils restent au Mexique.** *(They are staying in Mexico.)*
>
> **Mon ami vient aux États-Unis.** *(My friend is coming to the United States.)*
>
> **Nous avons des amis à Québec.** *(We have friends in Quebec.)*

Generally, countries that end in **-e** are feminine. Here are the exceptions:

> ✔ **le Cambodge** *(Cambodia)*
>
> ✔ **le Mexique** *(Mexico)*
>
> ✔ **le Zimbabwe** *(Zimbabwe)*

Countries that end in other vowels or consonants are masculine.

> ✔ **le Canada** *(Canada)*
>
> ✔ **l'Iran** *(Iran)*

En can also be used to express that someone is traveling around a country:

> **Il voyage en France en ce moment.** *(He's traveling around France at the moment.)*

Expressing "from" a place

The prepositions **de, du,** and **des** are used to express *from* before the names of places as follows:

- ✔ **de:** Use with feminine countries **(de France),** feminine continents **(d'Europe),** feminine provinces **(de Lorraine),** feminine islands **(de Sicile),** masculine countries beginning with a vowel **(d'Israël),** and cities **(de Paris).**

- ✔ **du (de + le):** Use with masculine countries beginning with a consonant **(du Mexique).**

- ✔ **des (de + les):** Use with plural countries **(des États-Unis).**

  Nous sommes de Suisse. *(We are from Switzerland.)*

  Il vient du Canada. *(He is from Canada.)*

  Arrivent-ils des États-Unis? *(Are they arriving from the United States?)*

If the feminine country begins with a vowel or mute h, **de** contracts to **d'.**

  Êtes-vous d'Égypte? *(Are you from Egypt?)*

Creating Modifiers

The prepositions **à (aux), de,** and **en** may be used after a noun to create an adjective.

Generally, **à (aux)** introduces a noun that expresses use, function, or the characteristic of an object or person.

  un verre à vin *(a wine glass)*

  un bateau à voiles *(a sailboat)*

  une boîte aux lettres *(a mailbox)*

  une fille aux cheveux blonds *(a girl with blond hair)*

A verb may follow **à** to describe the purpose of an object.

  une lotion à bronzer *(tanning lotion)*

Generally, **de (d')** introduces a noun that expresses the source, nature, or content of an object.

> **une statue de bois** *(a wooden statue)*

> **un maillot de bain** *(a bathing suit)*

> **une tasse de café** *(a cup of coffee)*

En may be used to describe something made of a precious metal (silver or gold, for example).

> **une montre en or** *(a gold watch)*

> **un bracelet en argent** *(a silver bracelet)*

Joining Verbs with Prepositions

Many French verbs need a preposition when they're followed by an infinitive. This section points out some of the more common verbs and the prepositions that go with them.

Verbs with à

Many French verbs require the preposition **à**. To use these verbs, just conjugate them, follow them with the preposition **à,** and then use an infinitive.

- ✔ **aider à** *(to help to)*
- ✔ **s'amuser à** *(to enjoy)*
- ✔ **apprendre à** *(to learn to)*
- ✔ **chercher à** *(to try to)*
- ✔ **commencer à** *(to begin to)*
- ✔ **continuer à** *(to continue to)*
- ✔ **se décider à** *(to make up one's mind to)*
- ✔ **s'habituer à** *(to get used to)*
- ✔ **hésiter à** *(to hesitate to)*
- ✔ **se mettre à** *(to begin to)*
- ✔ **penser à** *(to think about/of)*
- ✔ **se préparer à** *(to prepare to)*
- ✔ **réussir à** *(to succeed in)*
- ✔ **servir à** *(to be used for)*
- ✔ **tenir à** *(to insist upon)*

Elle apprend à nager. *(She's learning to swim.)*

Ce couteau sert à couper la viande. *(This knife is used for cutting meat.)*

The French infinitive after **à** often translates more naturally as the present participle in English.

Je m'amuse à regarder les touristes. *(I enjoy watching the tourists.)*

Verbs with de

Many French verbs require the preposition **de.** To use these verbs, just conjugate them, follow them with the preposition **de,** and then use an infinitive.

- ✔ **accepter de** *(to accept to)*
- ✔ **s'arrêter de** *(to stop)*
- ✔ **choisir de** *(to choose to)*
- ✔ **décider de** *(to decide to)*
- ✔ **se dépêcher de** *(to hurry to)*
- ✔ **empêcher de** *(to prevent from)*
- ✔ **essayer de** *(to try to)*
- ✔ **finir de** *(to finish)*
- ✔ **s'occuper de** *(to take care of)*
- ✔ **oublier de** *(to forget to)*
- ✔ **regretter de** *(to regret)*
- ✔ **refuser de** *(to refuse to)*
- ✔ **rêver de** *(to dream of)*
- ✔ **venir de** *(to have just)*

Elle finit de préparer le dîner. *(She finishes preparing dinner.)*

Ils viennent d'arriver. *(They just arrived.)*

À and **de** don't contract with the direct objects **le** and **les** (see Chapter 2).

Elle a appris à le faire. *(She learned to do it.)*

Il m'a dit de le faire. *(He told me to do it.)*

Verbs with à and de

Some verbs follow the pattern of **à** + person + **de** before the infinitive. These important verbs include:

- ✔ **commander à...de** *(to order someone to do something)*
- ✔ **conseiller à...de** *(to advise someone to do something)*
- ✔ **défendre à...de** *(to forbid someone to do something)*
- ✔ **demander à...de** *(to ask someone to do something)*
- ✔ **dire à...de** *(to tell someone to do something)*
- ✔ **ordonner à...de** *(to order someone to do something)*
- ✔ **permettre à...de** *(to permit someone to do something)*
- ✔ **promettre à...de** *(to promise something to someone)*

Il conseille à ses amis de voyager en France. *(He advises his friends to travel to France.)*

The verbs in the above list take an indirect object.

Elle promet à ses parents de faire ses devoirs. *(She promises <u>her parents</u> that she'll do her homework.)*

Elle leur promet de faire ses devoirs. *(She promises <u>them</u> that she'll do her homework.)*

Verbs with à and à

Two important verbs that may follow the pattern **à** + person + **à** are:

- ✔ **apprendre (à...à)** *(to teach [someone] to)*
- ✔ **enseigner (à...à)** *(to teach [someone] to)*

J'apprends (enseigne) à mon ami à plonger. *(I teach my friend to dive.)*

Verbs with other prepositions

All prepositions except **en** (which is followed by the present participle; see Chapter 3) may be followed by an infinitive. The most common are: **pour** *(to, in order to)*, **afin de** *(in order to)*, **avant de** *(before)*, **sans** *(without)*, and **au lieu de** *(instead of)*.

> **Il travaille pour gagner sa vie.** *(He works in order to earn a living.)*

> **Elle travaille sans regarder l'horloge.** *(She works without looking at the clock.)*

but

> **Nous mangeons en travaillant.** *(We work while eating.)*

Using verbs requiring no preposition

Some French verbs are followed directly by the infinitive, even though their English equivalents need a preposition. Here's a list to help you remember these verbs:

- ✔ **aimer (mieux)** *(to like/love) (to prefer)*
- ✔ **compter** *(to intend)*
- ✔ **désirer** *(to wish/ want)*
- ✔ **devoir** *(to have to)*
- ✔ **espérer** *(to hope)*
- ✔ **laisser** *(to let/allow)*
- ✔ **pouvoir** *(to be able to)*
- ✔ **préférer** *(to prefer)*
- ✔ **savoir** *(to know [how])*
- ✔ **valoir mieux** *(to be better)*
- ✔ **vouloir** *(to wish/ want)*

> **Je compte rester chez moi ce soir.** *(I intend to stay home tonight.)*

> **Elle aime mieux sortir.** *(She prefers to go out.)*

> **Savez-vous jouer du piano?** *(Do you know how to play the piano?)*

Chapter 6

Asking and Answering Questions

. . . .

. . . .

*I*n any language, being able to ask questions is important. Questions can range from the most simple (those requiring a yes or no answer) to more complex (those requiring detailed information, such as the date, time, and location for your party). Furthermore, you can use many styles to ask questions, ranging from informal, conversational styles (How ya doin'?) to the most formal styles, which you probably use mostly in writing and in polite situations (May I inquire as to your health?). Therefore, the way you ask a question depends on the circumstances and the environment you're in.

This chapter explains how to ask and answer different types of questions, and it provides all the interrogative vocabulary that goes along with them.

Presenting a Yes/No Question

French has four main ways to ask a question. They are as follows:

▮ ✔ **Intonation:** The most common and conversational way of asking a question, you simply raise your voice at the end of the sentence.

Tu regardes la télé? (*Are you watching television?*)

> ✔ **N'est-ce pas:** Another conversational way you can ask a question is to add **n'est-ce pas** at the end of the sentence.
>
> **Nous déjeunons ensemble, n'est-ce pas?** *(We're having lunch together, right?)*
>
> ✔ **Est-ce que:** The third conversational way of asking a question is by using **est-ce que** at the beginning of a sentence.
>
> **Est-ce que tu cherches tes clefs?** *(Are you looking for your keys?)*
>
> ✔ **Inversion:** The fourth and most formal way to ask a question is by inverting the subject pronoun and the verb and adding a hyphen.
>
> **Vas-tu au cinéma ce soir?** *(Are you going to the movies this evening?)*

The words *do* and *does* and sometimes *am, is,* and *are* don't translate from English into French. In French, these words are part of the meaning of the conjugated verb.

Ils viennent aujourd'hui? *(Are they coming today?)*

Inversion is a little bit more complicated than the informal methods. Inversion is also more formal, so in a business setting, it's the better option. Here's what it looks like when you make the changes stated above:

Est-il prêt? *(Is he ready?)*

Sait-il nager? *(Does he know how to swim?)*

You can invert only subject pronouns, not actual subjects. So when you ask a question with a subject, such as **Pierre** or **le chat** *(the cat),* you have to either replace the subject with a pronoun or start the question with the subject, followed by the inverted verb and subject pronoun.

Pierre est-il prêt? *(Is Pierre ready?)*

Le chat sait-il nager? *(Does the cat know how to swim?)*

When the verb ends in a vowel and is followed by a third-person singular pronoun **(il, elle, on),** you have to add **t** between the verb and pronoun.

Parle-t-elle français? *(Does she speak French?)*

A-t-on de l'argent? *(Do we have any money?)*

Inversion is a little trickier with reflexive verbs, because you have to consider the reflexive pronoun (see Chapter 3). Keep the reflexive pronoun exactly where it is — in front of the verb — and place the subject pronoun after the verb, as you can see in the following examples.

Se rase-t-il? *(Is he shaving?)*

Te lèves-tu de bonne heure? *(Do you wake up early?)*

Because in the **nous** and **vous** forms the subject pronouns and the reflexive pronouns look exactly the same, it can be difficult to know which is which. Just remember that the pronoun after the verb and the hyphen is the subject pronoun.

Nous aimons-nous? *(Do we love each other?)*

If a sentence has two verbs, you invert the conjugated verb with the subject pronoun.

Tu veux sortir. *(You want to go out.)*

Veux-tu sortir? *(Do you want to go out?)*

The same holds true for the passé composé (see Chapter 7), where you place the subject pronoun after the conjugated helping verb.

Es-tu sorti? *(Did you go out?)*

To ask a negative yes/no question using inversion, **ne** precedes the conjugated verb, and a negative expression (see the next section) follows the subject pronoun, like it does in the following examples.

Ne vendent-ils pas leur maison? *(Aren't they selling their house?)*

Ne parle-t-il jamais français? *(Doesn't he ever speak French?)*

> **Corinne ne veut-elle pas venir avec nous?** *(Doesn't Corinne want to come with us?)*
>
> **N'avez-vous rien mangé?** *(Haven't you eaten anything?)*

Answering a Yes/No question

Knowing how to ask questions is important. So is knowing how to answer questions — and how to understand other people's answers, too. This section gives you an overview of responding to different types of questions.

Being affirmative

Yes/no questions are not hard to answer. You can take the easy road and just answer **oui** *(yes)* or **non** *(no)*.

> **Est-ce qu'il est prêt? Oui.** *(Is he ready? Yes.)*
>
> **Avez-vous mangé? Non.** *(Have you eaten? No.)*

French has another word for yes, **si,** which you use when someone asks a question in the negative but you want to respond in the affirmative.

> **N'est-il pas prêt? Si (il est prêt).** *(Isn't he ready? Yes, [he is ready].)*
>
> **Tu ne veux pas savoir. Si (je veux savoir).** *(You don't want to know. Yes, [I do want to know].)*

Si *(yes)* never contracts, unlike **si** *(if)*, which contracts with **il: s'il vous plaît** *(if you please)*.

Being negative

Sometimes you have to refuse to do something or express your dislike for something or someone. To do this, you use the negative. This section explains different ways to be negative in French.

The most common French negatives are listed in the following table.

French	*Negative French Equivalent*
ne . . . pas	*not*
ne . . . ni . . . ni	*neither . . . nor*
ne . . . jamais	*never, (not) ever*
ne . . . personne	*no one, nobody*
ne . . . plus	*no longer*
ne . . . que	*only*
ne . . . rien	*nothing*

The negative consists of two parts: **ne,** which is placed before the conjugated verb and pronoun objects (direct, indirect, adverbial, and reflexive pronouns) and **pas** (or another negative word), which is generally placed after the conjugated verb (or the subject pronoun with inverted questions).

> **Je ne parle pas italien.** *(I do not speak Italian.)*
>
> **Ils ne mangent rien.** *(They aren't eating anything.)*
>
> **Nous ne nous amusons pas.** *(We are not having fun.)*
>
> **Ne s'est-il pas levé tôt?** *(Didn't he wake up early?)*

Note these special rules regarding the negative:

✔ Partitive articles **(du, de la, des)** and indefinite articles **(un, une, des)** change to **de (d'** before a vowel) after a negation. (See Chapter 2.)

> **J'ai un frère.** *(I have a brother.)*
>
> **Je n'ai pas de frère.** *(I don't have a brother.)*

✔ When the verb begins with a vowel or a mute **h,** drop the e of **ne** and add an apostrophe.

> **Elle n'habite pas à Paris.** *(She doesn't live in Paris.)*
>
> **Je n'ai pas fini.** *(I haven't finished.)*

✔ **Personne** and **rien** may be used as subjects and will precede the verb. **Ne** will retain its position before the conjugated verb.

> **Personne ne répond.** *(Nobody is answering.)*
>
> **Rien n'est trop difficile.** *(Nothing is too difficult.)*

✔ **Jamais,** when used independently, can mean *ever* or *never.* **Ne . . . jamais** means ***never.***

Avez-vous jamais voyagé en Europe? Non, jamais! *(Have you ever traveled to Europe? No, never!)*

✔ Both **ne** and the negative word or expression precede an infinitive, except for **personne,** which follows it (see the next bullet).

Il a choisi de ne rien dire. *(He chose to say nothing.)*

J'ai peur de ne pas réussir. *(I'm afraid of not succeeding.)*

✔ **Personne** (see Chapter 7) follows the past participle and the infinitive.

Nous n'avons rencontré personne au cinéma. *(We didn't meet anyone at the movies.)*

Je ne peux voir personne. *(I can't see anyone.)*

✔ **Que,** and each part of **ni . . . ni,** precede the words being stressed.

Je n'ai qu'une sœur. *(I have only one sister.)*

Je ne vais le dire qu'une fois. *(I'm only going to say it once.)*

Je n'ai ni frères ni sœurs. *(I have neither brothers nor sisters.)*

Il ne fait ni chaud ni froid. *(It's neither hot nor cold.)*

✔ **Ne** is always used with a verb, but the second part of the negative (except for **pas** and **plus**) may be used alone.

Qui est là? Personne. *(Who's there? Nobody.)*

Qu'est-ce que tu fais? Rien. *(What are you doing? Nothing.)*

When used in questions, some words require that you use negative words of opposite meaning in the responses. The following table presents these words.

If the question contains	*The negative answer should contain*
quelqu'un *(someone)*	**ne . . . personne** *(no one, nobody)*
quelque chose *(something)*	**ne . . . rien** *(nothing)*
toujours *(always)*	**ne . . . jamais** *(never)*
toujours *(still)*	**ne . . . plus** *(no longer)*

Here are examples:

> **Tu vois quelque chose?** *(Do you see something?)*
>
> **Je ne vois rien.** *(I don't see anything.)*
>
> **Elle fume toujours?** *(Does she still smoke?)*
>
> **Elle ne fume plus.** *(She no longer smokes.)*

Getting the Whole Story

Some questions ask for information, such as who, when, where, why, and how. French has three types of question words, and you need to understand the differences among them in order to get the information you need.

Understanding interrogative adjectives

You use the interrogative adjective **quel?** *(which?/what?)* before a noun when that noun may be counted or measured. **Quel?** varies and must agree in number and gender with the noun it describes.

	Masculine	*Feminine*
Singular	**quel?**	**quelle?**
Plural	**quels?**	**quelles?**

Here is an example of **quel?** in use:

> **Quelle chemise préfères-tu?** *(Which shirt do you prefer?)*
>
> **Quels livres est-ce que tu veux?** *(Which books do you want?)*

If you want to know what time something happens, use **à quelle heure?** *(at what time?)*.

Using interrogative adverbs

Interrogative adverbs ask for more information about something that happens. Important interrogative adverbs include:

- ✔ **comment** *(how)*
- ✔ **combien (de)** *(how much/many)*
- ✔ **quand** *(when)*
- ✔ **où** *(where)*
- ✔ **pourquoi** *(why)*

Here are a couple of these adverbs at work:

> **Comment as-tu fait ça?** *(How did you do that?)*
>
> **Quand vas-tu en France?** *(When are you going to France?)*

You can ask questions with interrogative adverbs and adjectives plus **est-ce que** by putting the question word at the beginning of the question, followed by **est-ce que,** the subject, and the verb.

> **Où est-ce que tu vas?** *(Where are you going?)*
>
> **Pourquoi est-ce qu'il aime le jazz?** *(Why does he like jazz?)*
>
> **Quand est-ce que Laure va arriver?** *(When is Laure going to arrive?)*

To ask a question using inversion, just put the interrogative word at the beginning and follow it with the inverted verb and subject.

> **Où vas-tu?** *(Where are you going?)*
>
> **Pourquoi aime-t-il le jazz?** *(Why does he like jazz?)*
>
> **Quand Laure va-t-elle arriver?** *(When is Laure going to arrive?)*

The question **Est-ce qu'il y a (Y a-t-il)** may be used to ask the question *is/are there?* Use *il y a (there is/are)* to answer the question.

Est-ce qu'il y a (Y a-t-il) un bon restaurant par ici? *(Is there a nice restaurant around here?)*

Il y a un bon restaurant à gauche. *(There's a good restaurant to the left.)*

Combien d'élèves est-ce qu'il y a (y a-t-il) dans cette classe? *(How many students are in this/that class?)*

Il y en a trente. *(There are thirty [of them].)*

Getting information with interrogative pronouns

Interrogative pronouns ask *who* **(qui)** or *what* **(que),** and because they're pronouns, you can't use them in front of a noun.

When you're asking a question with *who* or *what,* **est-ce que** gets more complicated. The following table shows you how this works.

Pronoun	Subject of Question	Object of Question
Who	Qui est-ce qui (or Qui)	Qui est-ce que
What	Qu'est-ce qui	Qu'est-ce que

The subjects **qui est-ce qui** and **qu'est-ce qui** are followed by verbs.

Qui est-ce qui est tombé? *(Who fell?)*

Qu'est-ce qui est tombé? *(What fell?)*

The objects **qui est-ce que** and **qu'est-ce que** are followed by nouns or pronouns.

Qui est-ce que tu cherches? *(Whom are you looking for?)*

Qu'est-ce que tu cherches? *(What are you looking for?)*

Que + est-ce que has to contract to **qu'est-ce que. Qui** doesn't contract with **est-ce que** or any other word.

Giving Information

This section is chock full of tips on how to answer questions that ask you for information in French.

- When you see a question with **comment?** *(how? what?)*, give the information or the explanation that's requested.

  Comment t'appelles-tu? *(What's your name?)*

  Suzanne. *(Suzanne.)*

- When you see a question with **combien (de)?** *(how much? how many?)*, you answer with a number, an amount, or a quantity (see Chapter 1).

  Combien coûte cette voiture? *(How much does this car cost?)*

  Vingt mille dollars. *($20,000)*

- When you see a question with **quand?** *(when?)*, you answer with a specific time or an expression of time.

  Quand est-ce que le film commence? *(When does the film begin?)*

  À trois heures et demie. *(At 3:30.)*

- When you see a question with **où?** *(where?)*, you answer with a place.

  Où vas-tu? *(Where are you going?)*

  À Genève. *(To Geneva.)*

- When you see a question with **pourquoi?** *(why?)*, answer with **parce que** *(because)* + a reason.

  Pourquoi ne travaille-t-elle pas? *(Why isn't she working?)*

  Parce qu'elle est malade. *(Because she's sick.)*

- When you see a question with **qui?** *(who? whom?)*, always answer by referring to a person.

  Qui parle au téléphone? Anne. *(Who's speaking on the phone? Anne.)*

If the question contains a preposition — **à, de, avec, pour,** and so on — you generally use that same preposition in the answer.

À qui écrivez-vous? *(To whom are you writing?)*

À mon petit ami. *(To my boyfriend.)*

Avec qui habites-tu? *(With whom do you live?)*

Avec mes parents. *(With my parents.)*

✓ When you see a question with **que?** *(what?)*, answer according to the situation. As with the preceding bullet, if the question contains a preposition, you must use that same preposition in the answer. Note that **que** becomes **quoi** after a preposition.

Que fais-tu? *(What are you doing?)*

Je lis. *(I'm reading.)*

Avec quoi écris-tu? *(With what are you writing?)*

Avec un crayon. *(With a pencil.)*

Chapter 7

Uncovering the Past

· ·

· ·

*W*hat's past is past. Or is it? The past tense can be a little murky in French. Sometimes, an action in the past is complete: It's done, over. In other cases, past action is a little more vague. It doesn't relate to a specific event but to a past action that was continuous, ongoing, or habitual — something you "used to do" or "were doing," for example, at no set period or time. In order to effectively understand and use the different past tenses in French, you need to become much more aware of their differences, and this chapter helps you do just that.

Dwelling on the Past with the Passé Composé

The compound past (the passé composé) recounts events that have already taken place and at a specific time in the past. You use the passé composé to express a completed action in the past. For example, with this tense you can recount what you have done and accomplished, where you've been, and the people you met yesterday, last week, last month, or even years ago.

You use the imperfect tense (the imparfait) to describe a continuous or habitual action in the past or an action that you did a nonspecific number of times.

The following sections show you how to form the passé composé and the imperfect tense for regular, irregular, and reflexive verbs, as well as the many ways you can correctly use the tenses.

Forming the passé composé of regular verbs

The passé composé has three meanings in English. For example, **J'ai parlé** means *I spoke, I have spoken,* and *I did speak.* To form the passé composé, you take the present tense of the helping verb (**avoir** or **être**) and select the appropriate past participle.

- ✔ avoir: j'ai, tu as, il/elle/on a, nous avons, vous avez, ils/elles ont

- ✔ être: je suis, tu es, il/elle/on est, nous sommes, vous êtes, ils/elles sont

To form the past participle of regular -er verbs, such as **parler** *(to speak)*, simply drop the **-er** and add **é (parlé)**. Check out the following tables that provide examples of regular verbs in the **passé composé**, conjugated in their entirety. Note that each has **avoir** as its helping verb.

Parler (to speak) in the passé composé	
j'ai parlé	nous avons parlé
tu as parlé	vous avez parlé
il/elle/on a parlé	ils/elles ont parlé

Nous avons parlé aux enfants. *(We spoke to the children.)*

Even verbs with spelling changes (see Chapter 3), such as **jeter** *(to throw)*, **acheter** *(to buy)*, **essayer** *(to try)*, **espérer** *(to hope)*, **appeler** *(to call)*, **lever** *(to raise)*, **placer** *(to place)*, and **manger** *(to eat)* have a regular past participle. Simply drop the **-er** from the infinitive and add **é**, like so: **jeté, acheté, essayé, espéré, appelé, levé, placé,** and **mangé.**

For the regular **-ir** verbs, such as **finir** *(to finish)*, simply drop the **–ir**, add **–i**, and voilà: **fini.**

Finir (to finish) in the passé composé	
j'ai fini	nous avons fini
tu as fini	vous avez fini
il/elle/on a fini	ils/elles ont fini

Elle a fini ses devoirs. *(She finished her homework.)*

Finally, for the regular **-re** verbs, like **vendre** *(to sell),* drop the
-re and add **u** to get **vendu.**

Vendre (to sell) in the passé composé	
j'ai vendu	nous avons vendu
tu as vendu	vous avez vendu
il/elle/on a vendu	ils/elles ont vendu

Les étudiants ont vendu leurs livres. *(The students sold
their books.)*

Forming the passé composé of irregular verbs

Many French verbs have an irregular past participle. In this
section, we group the verbs with an irregular past participle
according to their endings. Table 7-1 lists the irregular verbs
and their past participles that end in **u.**

Table 7-1	Irregular Verbs and Their Past Participles Ending in u
Infinitive	*Past Participle*
avoir *(to have)*	**eu**
boire *(to drink)*	**bu**
connaître *(to know)*	**connu**
courir *(to run)*	**couru**

(continued)

Table 7-1 *(continued)*

Infinitive	Past Participle
croire *(to believe)*	**cru**
devenir *(to become)*	**devenu**
devoir *(to owe, to have to)*	**dû**
falloir *(to be necessary, to have to)*	**fallu**
lire *(to read)*	**lu**
paraître *(to appear)*	**paru**
pleuvoir *(to rain)*	**plu**
pouvoir *(to be able to)*	**pu**
recevoir *(to receive)*	**reçu**
revenir *(to come back)*	**revenu**
savoir *(to know)*	**su**
tenir *(to hold)*	**tenu**
venir *(to come)*	**venu**
vivre *(to live)*	**vécu**
voir *(to see)*	**vu**
vouloir *(to want)*	**voulu**

Note that you create the past participle the same way for any verb that ends in **–venir** or **-tenir.**

Some past participles end in **t.** Table 7-2 shows those verbs along with their past participles.

Table 7-2   Irregular Verbs and Their Past Participles Ending in t

Infinitive	Past Participle
conduire *(to drive)*	**conduit**
construire *(to construct, to build)*	**construit**
couvrir *(to cover)*	**couvert**
dire *(to say)*	**dit**
écrire *(to write)*	**écrit**

Infinitive	Past Participle
faire *(to do, to make)*	fait
mourir *(to die)*	mort
offrir *(to offer)*	offert
ouvrir *(to open)*	ouvert
souffrir *(to suffer)*	souffert

Table 7-3 lists some irregular verbs whose past participles end in **s.** Note that you create the past participle the same way for any verb that ends in **-mettre** or **-prendre.**

Table 7-3   Irregular Verbs and Their Past Participles Ending in s

Infinitive	Past Participle
mettre *(to put, to place)*	mis
prendre *(to take)*	pris
apprendre *(to learn)*	appris

Some past participles of irregular verbs end in **i.** Table 7-4 shows the irregular verbs that have past participles ending in **i.**

Table 7-4   Irregular Verbs and Their Past Participles Ending in i

Infinitive	Past Participle
partir *(to leave)*	parti
rire *(to laugh)*	ri
sortir *(to go out)*	sorti
sourire *(to smile)*	souri
suivre *(to follow)*	suivi

Two other irregular verbs have an irregular past participle. Table 7-5 lists them.

Table 7-5   Irregular Verbs and Their Past Participles

Infinitive	Past Participle
être *(to be)*	**été**
naître *(to be born)*	**né**

Making agreements

Past participles agree in number and gender with a preceding direct object (noun or pronoun – see Chapter 2), if there is one. Depending on the direct object, you need to make the following changes to the past participle:

- ✔ If the preceding direct object is masculine singular, leave the past participle alone.
- ✔ If the preceding direct object is feminine singular, add an **e.**
- ✔ If the preceding direct object is masculine plural, add an **s.**
- ✔ If the preceding direct object is feminine plural, add an **-es.**

Check out the following examples to see how the past participle can change.

> **J'ai mis les fleurs dans le vase.** *(I put the flowers in the vase.)*
>
> **Je les ai mises dans le vase.** *(I put them in the vase.)*
>
> **La voiture que j'ai achetée était parfaite.** *(The car that I bought was perfect.)*

There's no agreement when the direct object follows the verb.

> **J'ai acheté une voiture parfaite.** *(I bought a perfect car.)*

Drop the vowel of **me, te, le,** and **la** and add an apostrophe when the verb begins with a vowel or a mute **h.** In the passé composé, when the auxiliary verb is **avoir,** this is always the case.

Ils m'ont prévenu(e). *(They warned me.)*

Je t'ai cherché(e). *(I looked for you.)*

Forming the passé composé of être verbs

Some specific verbs, many of them verbs of motion and verbs that aren't followed directly by a direct object, take **être** as their helping verb. Conjugate the verb **être** in the present tense and select the past participle of the verb you want.

To remember which verbs take **être** *(to be)*, picture a house. Many of the verbs that take **être** are what we call "door" verbs. You can go, come, return, enter, arrive, and pass through the door in the house of **être.** What about the staircase? You can go up, go down, and if you aren't careful, you can fall. Now picture the bed. Way before hospitals, people were born in the house and died in the house. These verbs take **être.**

The last types of verbs belonging to this category are all reflexive verbs, which take **être** as their helping verb.

You form the passé composé of **être** verbs the same way as **avoir** verbs. You conjugate the verb **être** in the present tense and select the past participle of the verb.

Il est arrivé à 9 heures. *(He arrived at 9 o'clock.)*

Elle s'est levée tard. *(She woke up late.)*

Table 7-6 shows the verbs that use **être** when forming the passé composé, along with their past participles.

Table 7-6   Verbs Taking Être in the Passé Composé

Infinitive	Past Participle
aller *(to go)*	**allé**
arriver *(to arrive)*	**arrivé**
descendre* *(to go downstairs, to descend)*	**descendu**
devenir *(to become)*	**devenu**

(continued)

Table 7-6 *(continued)*

Infinitive	Past Participle
entrer *(to enter)*	**entré**
monter* *(to go upstairs, to climb)*	**monté**
mourir *(to die)*	**mort**
naître *(to be born)*	**né**
partir *(to leave)*	**parti**
passer* *(to pass, to spend)*	**passé**
rentrer* *(to go home)*	**rentré**
rester *(to stay)*	**resté**
retourner* *(to return)*	**retourné**
revenir *(to come back)*	**revenu**
sortir* *(to go out)*	**sorti**
tomber *(to fall)*	**tombé**
venir *(to come)*	**venu**

Note: The verbs with asterisks can take either **avoir** or **être**. They take **avoir** when they're followed by a direct object and they take **être** when they aren't followed by a direct object.

> **Elle est sortie et elle a sorti son parapluie.** *(She went out and she took out her umbrella.)*

The past participle of **être** verbs agrees with the subject. Thus,

- ✔ If the subject is masculine singular, leave the past participle alone.
- ✔ If the subject is feminine singular, add an **e** to the past participle.
- ✔ If the subject is masculine plural, add an **s.**
- ✔ If the subject is feminine plural, add an **es.**

> **Nous sommes partis à midi.** *(We left at noon.)*

When the reflexive pronoun is an indirect object (because there is a direct object in the sentence), the past participle remains unchanged.

> **Elle s'est lavée.** *(She washed herself.)*
>
> **Elle s'est lavé les mains.** *(She washed her hands.)*

Using the passé composé

You use the **passé composé** to refer to one of three things:

✔ Something that was entirely completed in the past

> **Je suis allé à la banque hier.** *(I went to the bank yesterday.)*
>
> **Est-il arrivé avant la fête?** *(Did he arrive before the party?)*

✔ Something that happened a certain number of times in the past

> **J'ai visité la tour Eiffel trois fois.** *(I've visited the Eiffel Tower three times.)*
>
> **Combien de fois lui as-tu téléphoné?** *(How many times did you call him?)*

✔ A series of actions that occurred one after another in the past

> **Je me suis levé, j'ai déjeuné et je suis parti avant 7h00.** *(I got up, had breakfast, and left before 7 a.m.)*
>
> **Quand nous avons entendu les cris, nous avons téléphoné à la police.** *(When we heard the screams, we called the police.)*

When you express something negative in the passé composé, **ne** goes in front of the helping verb, and the second part of the negative structure goes after it. The only exception is **personne,** which goes after the past participle.

> **Je n'ai pas pleuré.** *(I didn't cry.)*
>
> **Je n'ai vu personne.** *(I didn't see anyone.)*

When you ask a question with inversion (see Chapter 6), you invert just the subject pronoun and the auxiliary verb and put the past participle after that.

> **As-tu mangé?** *(Have you eaten?)*
>
> **À qui a-t-il parlé?** *(Whom did he talk to?)*

Reminiscing with the Imperfect

You use the imperfect tense to describe a continuous or habitual action in the past, or an action that you did a nonspecific number of times. This section explains how to conjugate regular and irregular verbs in the imperfect, how and when to use the imperfect, the difference between the imperfect and passé composé, and how to use them together.

To conjugate regular verbs in the imperfect, just find the present-tense **nous** form of the verb, drop **-ons,** and add the imperfect endings. This rule applies to all regular, irregular, spelling change, and reflexive verbs. (Check out Chapter 3 for more about the present tense.) The endings are all the same, even for irregular verbs. The imperfect endings are as follows:

je -ais	nous -ions
tu -ais	vous -iez
il/elle/on -ait	ils/elles -aient

So the imperfect tense conjugations for a regular verb are as follows.

parler (to speak)	
Present-tense **nous** form: **parlons**	
je parlais	nous parlions
tu parlais	vous parliez
il/elle/on parlait	ils/elles parlaient

Il parlait à ses parents. *(He was speaking to his parents.)*

finir (to finish)	
Present-tense **nous** form: **finissons**	
je finissais	nous finissions
tu finissais	vous finissiez
il/elle/on finissait	ils/elles finissaient

Je finissais mon déjeuner. *(I was finishing my lunch.)*

vendre (to sell)	
Present-tense **nous** form: **vendons**	
je vendais	nous vendions
tu vendais	vous vendiez
il/elle/on vendait	ils/elles vendaient

Nous vendions notre maison. *(We were selling our house.)*

What if the stem of the verb in the **nous** form ends in an *i*, like **étudier** *(to study)*? Just keep the **i** and add the endings: **j'étudiais, tu étudiais, il/elle/on étudiait, nous étudiions, vous étudiiez, ils/elles étudiaient.**

For verbs that end in **-cer** and **–ger,** you need to add a cedilla to the **c,** and add an **e** after the **g** respectively for all imperfect conjugations except those for **nous** and **vous.**

je commençais, tu commençais, il/elle commençait, nous commencions, vous commenciez, ils/elles commençaient

je mangeais, tu mangeais, il/elle/on mangeait, nous mangions, vous mangiez, ils/elles mangeaient

To create the imperfect tense of irregular verbs, simply take their **nous** present-tense form, drop the **-ons,** and add the appropriate endings. Check out Table 7-7, which lists several irregular verbs in their present-tense **nous** form.

Table 7-7	Nous Forms of Irregular Verbs	
Infinitive	*Nous form*	*Stem*
aller *(to go)*	**Nous allons**	**all-**
avoir *(to have)*	**Nous avons**	**av-**
boire *(to drink)*	**Nous buvons**	**buv-**
croire *(to believe)*	**Nous croyons**	**croy-**
devoir *(to owe, to have to, must)*	**Nous devons**	**dev-**
dire *(to say)*	**Nous disons**	**dis-**
écrire *(to write)*	**Nous écrivons**	**écriv-**
faire *(to do, to make)*	**Nous faisons**	**fais-**
lire *(to read)*	**Nous lisons**	**lis-**
mettre *(to put, to place)*	**Nous mettons**	**mett-**
ouvrir *(to open)*	**Nous ouvrons**	**ouvr-**
partir *(to leave)*	**Nous partons**	**part-**
pouvoir *(to be able to)*	**Nous pouvons**	**pouv-**
prendre *(to take)*	**Nous prenons**	**pren-**
recevoir *(to receive)*	**Nous recevons**	**recev-**
venir *(to come)*	**Nous venons**	**ven-**
voir *(to see)*	**Nous voyons**	**voy-**
vouloir *(to want)*	**Nous voulons**	**voul-**

French does have one, single irregular verb that's also irregular in the imperfect: **être.** You use the stem **ét-** and add the imparfait endings to that.

être (to be)	
j'étais	**nous étions**
tu étais	**vous étiez**
il/elle/on était	**ils/elles étaient**

Vous étiez en retard. *(You were late.)*

You can use the imperfect to express a number of things that happened or existed in the past. Here's what to express with the imperfect:

✔ Something that happened an unknown number of times, especially habitual actions.

Je visitais le Louvre tous les jours. *(I visited/used to visit the Louvre every day.)*

L'année dernière, il préparait le dîner régulièrement. *(Last year, he prepared dinner regularly.)*

✔ States of being and descriptions.

Quand j'étais petit, j'aimais danser. *(When I was little, I liked/used to like to dance.)*

La voiture faisait du bruit. *(The car was making noise.)*

✔ Actions or states of being with no specific beginning or end.

Je regardais la télé pendant le petit déjeuner. *(I watched/was watching TV during breakfast.)*

Nous avions besoin de tomates. *(We needed tomatoes.)*

✔ Two things that were happening at the same time.

Il travaillait et j'étudiais. *(He was working and I was studying.)*

Je lisais pendant que mon frère jouait au tennis. *(I was reading while my brother was playing tennis.)*

✔ Background information and actions/states of being that got interrupted. The interruption is expressed with the passé compose.

Travaillais-tu quand je t'ai téléphoné? *(Were you working when I called you?)*

J'avais faim, donc j'ai acheté un sandwich. *(I was hungry, so I bought a sandwich.)*

✔ Wishes, suggestions, and conditions after **si** *(if)*.

Si seulement elle venait avec nous. *(If only she were coming with us.)*

Et si on allait au ciné ce soir? *(How about going to the movies tonight?)*

Si j'étais riche, je ferais le tour du monde. *(If I were rich, I would travel the world.)*

In the third example, **je ferais** is the conditional of **faire** *(to do, to make)*. See Chapter 9 to read about the conditional.

➤ Time, date, and age.

> **C'était lundi.** *(It was Monday.)*
>
> **Tu étais trop jeune**. *(You were too young.)*
>
> **Il y avait/était une fois** . . . *(Once upon a time . . .)*

The English translation of the imperfect is: was doing something, used to do something, or would do something in the past, where *would* means "used to." This isn't the same as the would of the conditional tense (see Chapter 9).

> **Quand j'habitais à Paris, je prenais souvent le métro.**
> *(When I lived in Paris, I would [used to] often take the train).*

Comparing the Passé Composé and the Imperfect

The imperfect and the passé composé express the past differently, so only by working together can they can fully express what happened in the past. In order for you to use the right one at the right time, you need to know what each tense describes. Table 7-8 spells out their differences.

Table 7-8	Functions of the Imperfect and the Passé Composé
Uses of the Imparfait	**Uses of the Passé Composé**
What was going on with no indication of when it started or ended	Things that happened with a definite beginning and/or end
Habitual or repeated actions	Single events
Simultaneous actions	Sequential actions
Something that got interrupted	Actions that interrupted something
Background information	Changes in physical or mental states
General descriptions	

Certain terms can help you decide whether to use the imperfect or passé composé. The following terms are usually used with the imparfait:

- ✔ **toujours** *(always)*
- ✔ **d'habitude, normalement** *(usually)*
- ✔ **en général** *(in general)*
- ✔ **généralement** *(generally)*
- ✔ **souvent** *(often)*
- ✔ **parfois, quelquefois** *(sometimes)*
- ✔ **de temps en temps** *(from time to time)*
- ✔ **chaque semaine, mois, année . . .** *(every week, month, year . . .)*
- ✔ **tous les jours, toutes les semaines** *(every day, every week)*
- ✔ **le week-end** *(on the weekends)*
- ✔ **le lundi, le mardi . . .** *(on Mondays, on Tuesdays . . .)*
- ✔ **le matin, le soir** *(in the mornings, in the evenings)*

  Quand j'étais jeune j'allais toujours à la plage. *(When I was young I always went to the beach.)*

These terms tell you that you probably should use the passé composé:

- ✔ **une fois, deux fois, trois fois . . .** *(once, twice, three times . . .)*
- ✔ **plusieurs fois** *(several times)*
- ✔ **soudainement** *(suddenly)*
- ✔ **tout d'un coup** *(all of a sudden)*
- ✔ **quand** *(when)*
- ✔ **un jour** *(one day)*
- ✔ **un week-end** *(one weekend)*
- ✔ **lundi, mardi . . .** *(on Monday, on Tuesday . . .)*

  Lundi soir je suis allé au cinéma. *(Monday night I went to the movies.)*

Chapter 8

Foreseeing the Future

In This Chapter

▶ Employing the future in three ways

▶ Forming the future of regular and irregular verbs

▶ Using the future

*W*ith the future tense you can describe events that will occur either at a specific time or an unspecified time in the future. In this chapter, you can discover how to form the future tense and how to use it with various expressions.

Speaking about the Future by Using the Present

The future tense can have a slightly formal feel to it. If you want to lighten your conversation and make it a tad less formal, you can talk about the future in a couple of other ways, especially if you're discussing something that'll happen soon (like what you'll do to your little brother if he changes the channel one more time). This section helps you add a little casualness to your words when referring to the future.

Employing the present to express the future

In both French and English, you can use the present tense to talk about something that's in the future. When you're going to do something in just a few minutes or in the next few days, the present tense helps bring that event just a little closer. It's slightly less formal than the future.

> **Je vais à la plage demain.** *(I'm going to the beach tomorrow.)*

> **Nous partons dans dix minutes.** *(We're leaving in ten minutes.)*

Using the near future

You can talk about the near future with the present tense of **aller** + the infinitive. This near future construction is equivalent to *to be going to do* something in English. Like the present tense, the near future is just slightly informal and tends to be a good choice when what's going to happen is going to happen soon.

aller (to go)	
je vais	nous allons
tu vas	vous allez
il/elle/on va	ils/elles vont

> **Il va travailler pendant toute la journée.** *(He's going to work all day.)*

> **Alexandre et Laurent vont être déçus.** *(Alexandre and Laurent are going to be disappointed.)*

With reflexive verbs (see Chapter 3), the reflexive pronoun goes in front of the infinitive.

> **Nous allons nous promener sur la plage.** *(We're going to take a walk on the beach.)*

> **Vas-tu t'habiller?** *(Are you going to get dressed?)*

Object and adverbial pronouns also precede the infinitive.

> **Je vais le faire demain.** *(I'm going to do it tomorrow.)*

> **Ils vont en avoir envie.** *(They're going to want some.)*

Conquering the Future Tense

Expressing the future in French can be a snap. In the future, all verbs take the same endings (no matter what the future stem is).

Creating the future tense for regular **-er, -ir,** and **-re** verbs is a piece of cake. All you have to do is take the infinitive of the verb, which serves as the stem, and add the appropriate endings. Remember that the future stem of all verbs, be they regular or irregular, always ends in **-r.** So for **-er** and **-ir** verbs, just add the endings. For **-re** verbs, drop the **e** and then add the appropriate endings.

Future Tense Verb Endings	
je -ai	nous -ons
tu -as	vous -ez
il/elle/on -a	ils/elles -ont

Do these future endings look familiar? If you're familiar with the present conjugation of **avoir** *(to have),* you may notice a similarity.

The following are the three categories of regular verbs — **-er, -ir,** and **-re** — in the future tense.

parler (to speak)	
je parlerai	nous parlerons
tu parleras	vous parlerez
il/elle/on parlera	ils/elles parleront

Je parlerai à l'agent de voyage demain. *(I will speak to the travel agent tomorrow.)*

finir (to finish)	
je finirai	nous finirons
tu finiras	vous finirez
il/elle/on finira	ils/elles finiront

Ils finiront leurs études l'année prochaine. (*They will finish their studies next year.*)

vendre (to sell)	
je vendrai	nous vendrons
tu vendras	vous vendrez
il/elle/on vendra	ils/elles vendront

Nous vendrons nos livres à la fin du semestre. (*We will sell our books at the end of the semester.*)

Forming the future of spelling-change verbs

Some **-er** verbs have a mute e in the infinitive. When you conjugate these types of verbs in the present tense, some spelling changes are required in order to pronounce the mute e. You either add an accent grave to the e, like so **(è),** or you double the consonant after the mute e. (See Chapter 3 for a list of these types of verbs.) The same types of changes occur to these verbs in the future tense, as shown in Tables 8-1 and 8-2.

Table 8-1   Accent Grave (è) Spelling-Change in Verbs in the Future Tense

Verb	Future Tense Stem
acheter *(to buy)*	**achèter-**
mener *(to lead)*	**mèner-**
(se) lever *(to rise/to stand up)*	**(se) lèver-**

J'achèterai mon billet la semaine prochaine. *(I will buy my ticket next week.)*

Table 8-2	Double Consonant Spelling-Change in Verbs in the Future Tense
Verb	**Future Tense Stem**
jeter *(to throw)*	jetter-
(s') appeler *(to call/to call oneself/to be named)*	(s') appeller-

Elle appellera son chien. *(She will call her dog.)*

Spelling-change verbs like **commencer** *(to begin)* and **manger** *(to eat)* have no spelling change in the future tense. Just take the infinitive and add the appropriate ending: **-ai, -as, -a, -ons, -ez,** or **-ont.**

Nous commencerons dans cinq minutes. *(We'll begin in five minutes.)*

Verbs whose infinitive form ends in **-yer** change to **-ier** before the endings; we show you examples of these verbs in Table 8-3. (An exception is the verb **envoyer** *[to send],* whose future stem is **enverr-.**)

Table 8-3	-yer to -ier Spelling-Change Verbs in the Future Tense
Verb	**Future Tense Stem**
employer *(to use)*	emploier-
essayer *(to try)*	essaier-
nettoyer *(to clean)*	nettoier-

Nous nettoierons notre chambre. *(We will clean our room.)*

Verbs that end in **-ayer** have an optional y-to-i stem change in the future. There is absolutely no difference between these two conjugations — they are equally acceptable, though you should be consistent. Just use the infinitive **payer** or the stem-changed infinitive **paier** and add the ending **-ai, -as, -a, -ons, -ez,** or **-ont.**

> **Je payerai (paierai) demain.** *(I'll pay tomorrow.)*

The **é*-er** verbs don't have a stem change in the future tense; don't change the accents in infinitives like **espérer** *(to hope)*, **préférer** *(to prefer)*, and **répéter** *(to repeat)*.

> **Tu répéteras après le professeur.** *(You will repeat after the professor.)*

Forming the future of irregular verbs

Some verbs have an irregular future stem. However, the endings remain the same. Table 8-4 lists the verbs with the irregular future tense stem.

Table 8-4	Irregular Future Tense Verbs
Irregular Verb	*Future Tense Stem*
aller *(to go)*	**ir-**
avoir *(to have)*	**aur-**
courir *(to run)*	**courr-**
devenir *(to become)*	**deviendr-**
devoir *(to owe, to have to)*	**devr-**
envoyer *(to send)*	**enverr-**
être *(to be)*	**ser-**
faire *(to do, to make)*	**fer-**
falloir *(to have to, must)*	**faudr-**
mourir *(to die)*	**mourr-**
pleuvoir *(to rain)*	**pleuvr-**
pouvoir *(to be able to)*	**pourr-**
recevoir *(to receive)*	**recevr-**

Irregular Verb	Future Tense Stem
revenir *(to come back)*	**reviendr-**
savoir *(to know)*	**saur-**
tenir *(to hold)*	**tiendr-**
valoir *(to be worth)*	**vaudr-**
venir *(to come)*	**viendr-**
voir *(to see)*	**verr-**
vouloir *(to want)*	**voudr-**

J'irai à la plage. *(I will go to the beach.)*

Elle saura la réponse bientôt. *(She will know the answer soon.)*

Using the Future

After you become comfortable creating the future tense, you'll become familiar with some expressions and when to use them. Here, we list some time expressions, which provide more specific information as to when in the future the event will take place. You can place them either in the beginning or at the end of the sentence.

- ✔ **demain** *(tomorrow)*
- ✔ **demain matin** *(tomorrow morning)*
- ✔ **demain après-midi** *(tomorrow afternoon)*
- ✔ **demain soir** *(tomorrow evening)*
- ✔ **la semaine prochaine** *(next week)*
- ✔ **le mois prochain** *(next month)*
- ✔ **l'année prochaine** *(next year)*
- ✔ **lundi prochain** *(next Monday)*
- ✔ **plus tard** *(later)*

(Demain) Ils passeront l'examen demain. *(They will take the test tomorrow.)*

In French, you also use the future tense after certain conjunctions when they indicate something that is going to happen in the future. Those conjunctions include the following:

- **après que** *(after)*
- **aussitôt que** *(as soon as)*
- **dès que** *(as soon as)*
- **lorsque** *(when)*
- **quand** *(when)*

> **Je te téléphonerai quand j'arriverai à l'hôtel.** *(I will call you when I arrive at the hotel.)*

> **Il le fera dès qu'il finira son travail.** *(He'll do it as soon as he finishes his work.)*

You use the present tense after these expressions in English, but in French, the future is required because the action after the expression has not yet occurred.

You can also use the future tense to talk about something that will happen in the future if a certain condition is met. Remember: if you use the future tense in the main clause, the condition after **si** *(if)* (see Chapter 9) has to be in the present tense.

> **J'irai en France si tu viens avec moi.** *(I will go to France if you come with me.)*

> **Si tu viens chez moi, nous regarderons le film ensemble.** *(If you come to my house, we'll watch the movie together.)*

You can also give polite requests using the future tense — this is more polite than using the imperative: it's a request more than a demand. (See Chapter 9 for more information about commands.)

> **Vous me suivrez, s'il vous plaît.** *(Follow me, please.)*

Chapter 9

Recognizing Verb Moods

• •

In This Chapter

▶ Issuing commands

▶ Getting subjective with the present subjunctive

▶ Speculating with the present perfect subjunctive

▶ Using the conditional

• •

*I*n other chapters in this book, we cover verb tenses (past, present, and future). In this chapter, we explain different moods of verbs. A *mood* is a verb form that indicates how the speaker feels about the action of the verb, whether it is real (the indicative mood), conditional (the conditional mood), subjective (the subjunctive mood), or a command (the imperative mood).

   ✔ The *indicative mood,* the most commonly used, generally states a fact and requires the present, past, or future tense. (See Chapters 3, 7, and 8 for more on these tenses.)

   ✔ The *imperative mood* requires a command.

   ✔ The *subjunctive* is a mood that shows wishing, wanting, emotion, need, or doubt (among other things).

   ✔ The conditional mood indicates what *would* happen under certain circumstances.

In this chapter, we focus on commands, the present subjunctive, and the conditional moods.

Giving Orders with the Imperative

The technical term for giving commands or orders is the *imperative.* You usually give orders in English as well as in French by using the verb directly and eliminating the "you" or "we" subject of the command (**tu, vous,** or **nous**), which is understood. In the following sections, we show you how to form commands with regular verbs.

Forming affirmative commands

The commands come from the **tu, vous,** and **nous** forms of the present tense (see Chapter 3). Note that the subject pronouns are never used in the command, just their verb forms.

Here's how commands are formed for regular **–er, -ir,** and **–re** verbs:

Familiar (tu)		Polite (vous)		Let's (nous)	
Parle!	*(Speak!)*	Parlez!	*(Speak!)*	Parlons!	*(Let's speak!)*
Finis!	*(Finish!)*	Finissez!	*(Finish!)*	Finissons!	*(Let's finish!)*
Attends!	*(Wait!)*	Attendez!	*(Wait!)*	Attendons!	*(Let's wait!)*

You drop the **s** from the **tu** form of regular verbs, irregular **–er** verbs like **aller** *(to go),* and **-ir** verbs, which are conjugated like regular **-er** verbs — like **ouvrir** *(to open),* **souffrir** *(to suffer),* and **offrir** *(to offer).* The **s** reappears when the verb is followed by the pronouns **y** or **en** for pronunciation reasons.

> **Parle-moi!** *(Speak to me!)*
>
> **Va chez le docteur!** *(Go to the doctor!)*

but

Parles-en! *(Speak about it!)*

Vas-y! *(Go there!)*

The negative command follows the standard rule of dropping the **–s.**

N'en parle pas! *(Don't speak about it!)*

N'y va pas! *(Don't go there!)*

The **nous** and **vous** forms don't have any changes.

Forming negative commands

In a negative command, **ne** precedes the verb and any of its objects and the second negative element follows the verb, and a preposition, if there is one.

Ne le fais pas! *(Don't do it!)*

Ne lui écris jamais! *(Never write to him!)*

Ne parle à personne! *(Don't speak to anyone!)*

Three irregular verbs, however, also have highly irregular imperative forms.

Infinitive	*Familiar (tu form)*	*Polite (vous form)*	*First person plural (nous form)*
avoir	**Aie** *(Have)*	**Ayez** *(Have)*	**Ayons** *(Let's have)*
être	**Sois** *(Be)*	**Soyez** *(Be)*	**Soyons** *(Let's be)*
savoir	**Sache** *(Know)*	**Sachez** *(Know)*	**Sachons** *(Let's know)*

N'aie pas peur! *(Don't be afraid!)*

Sois sage! *(Be good!)*

Sachez bien les règles! *(Know the rules well!)*

For the verb **vouloir,** you mostly use the **veuillez** form when giving commands, and you usually follow it with the infinitive.

This word is a polite way to give commands and is often translated as *please.*

> **Veuillez entrer.** *(Please come in.)*

When the infinitive is negative, the **ne** and **pas** are placed together and precede the infinitive.

> **Veuillez ne pas fumer!** *(Please don't smoke!)*

Forming reflexive commands

You eliminate the subject pronoun in the imperative form, but you still have to keep the reflexive pronoun when you're working with reflexive verbs (see Chapter 3). In the affirmative imperative, the reflexive pronoun follows the verb and is joined to it with a hyphen. In the negative command, the reflexive pronoun precedes the verb. The reflexive pronoun **te** becomes **toi** in the affirmative but then returns to **te** in the negative.

If the verb begins with a vowel or a mute h, drop the **e** from **te** and add an apostrophe.

> **Habille-toi!** *(Get dressed!)*
>
> **Ne t'habille pas!** *(Don't get dressed!)*
>
> **Dépêchez-vous!** *(Hurry up!)*
>
> **Ne vous dépêchez pas!** *(Don't hurry!)*
>
> **Maquillons-nous!** *(Let's put on makeup!)*
>
> **Ne nous maquillons pas!** *(Let's not put on makeup!)*

Understanding the Present Subjunctive

The subjunctive mood indicates subjectivity — the speaker may want something to happen or think it's important for something to happen, but the subjunctive tells you that something may or may not actually happen. The present tense, in contrast, generally states a fact or the way something actually is. Whereas the indicative mood expresses an objective reality, the subjunctive mood expresses the speaker's or writer's subjective points of view, emotions, fears, and doubts. This section tells you all about the subjunctive: how to form it, and when to use it.

Because French doesn't have a future subjunctive, the present subjunctive expresses the future as well as the present and can be translated in English in the tense that makes the most sense.

Forming the present subjunctive of regular verbs

To form the present subjunctive, start from the third-person plural of the indicative, the **ils/elles** form, drop the **-ent** to form the stem, and add the following endings: **-e, -es, -e, -ions, -iez,** or **-ent,** as shown in Table 9-1.

Table 9-1	The Present Subjunctive Endings of Regular Verbs		
	-er verbs	*-ir verbs*	*-ir verbs*
ils form of present tense	**parlent** *(they speak)*	**finissent** *(they finish)*	**vendent** *(they sell)*
je	parl**e**	finiss**e**	vend**e**
tu	parl**es**	finiss**es**	vend**es**
il, elle, on	parl**e**	finiss**e**	vend**e**
nous	parl**ions**	finiss**ions**	vend**ions**
vous	parl**iez**	finiss**iez**	vend**iez**
ils, elles	parl**ent**	finiss**ent**	vend**ent**

Here are some examples of these verbs in the subjunctive:

> **Il est essentiel que nous parlions au directeur.** *(It is essential that we speak to the director.)*

> **Il est possible que je finisse à 5 heures.** *(It's possible that I will finish at 5 o'clock.)*

Nous sommes surpris que tu vendes ta maison. *(We are surprised that you are selling your house.)*

As strange as it looks and sounds, you add the regular subjunctive **-ions** and **–iez** endings to verbs whose subjunctive stem already ends in **–i.** These verbs include **étudier** *(to study)*, **rire** *(to laugh)*, and **sourire** *(to smile)*. For example: the stem (from **ils étudient**) is **étudi-.** The subjunctive forms are: **j'étudie, tu étudies, il/elle/on étudie, nous étudiions, vous étudiiez, ils/elles étudient.**

Il est important que nous étudiions. *(It is important that we study.)*

Coping with changes

Certain verbs have two different stems just as they did in the present tense: one for the **je, tu, il/elle/on,** and **ils/elles** forms and another for the **nous** and **vous** forms. The way to remember these verbs is to refer to their present indicative forms.

Table 9-2 shows verbs with two stems, which include some irregular verbs and all verbs with spelling changes ending in **eler, eter, yer, ayer,** e+ consonant +**er, and é** + consonant + **er.**

Table 9-2	Verbs with Two Subjunctive Stems		
Infinitive	*Meaning*	*je, tu, il, elle stem of subjunctive*	*nous, vous stem of subjunctive*
appeler	*(to call)*	**appell-**	**appel-**
acheter	*(to buy)*	**achèt-**	**achet-**
boire	*(to drink)*	**boiv-**	**buv-**
croire	*(to believe)*	**croi-**	**croy-**
devoir	*(to have to, to owe)*	**doiv-**	**dev-**
ennuyer	*(to bother)*	**ennui-**	**ennuy-**
envoyer	*(to send)*	**envoi-**	**envoy-**

Infinitive	Meaning	je, tu, il, elle stem of subjunctive	nous, vous stem of subjunctive
employer	(to use)	emploi-	employ-
jeter	(to throw)	jett-	jet-
mener	(to lead)	mèn-	men-
mourir	(to die)	meur-	mour-
payer	(to pay)	pai-(pay-)	pay-
préférer	(to prefer)	préfèr-	préfér-
prendre	(to take)	prenn-	pren-
recevoir	(to receive)	reçoiv-	recev-
répéter	(to repeat)	répèt-	répét-
tenir	(to hold)	tienn-	ten-
venir	(to come)	vienn-	ven-
voir	(to see)	voi-	voy-

Here are some examples:

Nous sommes heureux que vous veniez. *(We are happy that you're coming.)*

Il est possible qu'ils reçoivent la coupe. *(It is possible that they will receive the cup.)*

You conjugate similar verbs, like **tenir** *(to hold)* and its compounds, the same way. These include **appartenir** *(to belong)*, **contenir** *(to contain)*, **maintenir** *(to maintain)*, **obtenir** *(to obtain)*, **retenir** *(to retain)*, **revenir** *(to come back)*, and **soutenir** *(to support)*.

Conjugating irregular verbs

Faire, pouvoir, and **savoir** have a single irregular stem in the subjunctive and use the regular subjunctive endings.

faire *(to make, to do):* **je fasse, tu fasses, il/elle/on fasse, nous fassions, vous fassiez, ils/elles fassent**

pouvoir *(to be able to, can):* **je puisse, tu puisses, il/elle/on puisse, nous puissions, vous puissiez, ils/elles puissent**

> **savoir** *(to know [how])*: **je sache, tu saches, il/elle/on sache, nous sachions, vous sachiez, ils/elles sachent**

Here are some examples:

> **Il est bon que tu le fasses.** *(It's good [that] you're doing it.)*
>
> **Elle ne croit pas que je puisse nager.** *(She doesn't believe that I can swim.)*
>
> **Il est important que vous sachiez lire.** *(It's important for you to know how to read.)*

Aller and **vouloir** have two irregular stems in the subjunctive and use the regular subjunctive endings.

> **aller** *(to go):* **j'aille, tu ailles, il/elle/on aille, nous allions, vous alliez, ils/elles aillent**
>
> **vouloir** *(to want):* **je veuille, tu veuilles, il/elle/on veuille, nous voulions, vous vouliez, ils/elles veuillent**

For example:

> **Veux-tu que j'aille avec toi?** *(Do you want me to go with you?)*
>
> **Il est possible qu'elles veuillent partir tôt.** *(It's possible that they want to leave early.)*

Finally, **avoir** and **être** have completely irregular subjunctive conjugations. Also note that the **tu, nous,** and **vous** subjunctive forms of **avoir, être,** and **savoir** are similar to the imperative forms mentioned previously in this chapter.

> **avoir** *(to have):* **j'aie, tu aies, il/elle/on ait, nous ayons, vous ayez, ils/elles aient**
>
> **être** *(to be):* **je sois, tu sois, il/elle/on soit, nous soyons, vous soyez, ils/elles soient**
>
> **Je suis heureux que tu aies une nouvelle voiture.** *(I'm happy [that] you have a new car.)*
>
> **Nous avons peur qu'elle soit malade.** *(We're afraid that she's sick.)*

Putting the present subjunctive to use

The most important thing to understand about the subjunctive mood is that it expresses subjectivity. When a desire, doubt, emotion, judgment, or necessity is expressed in one clause of a sentence, you have to use the subjunctive in the other clause to show that the action of the verb is not necessarily a fact, but rather is based on the subjective notion in the phrase that precedes it. The verb in the subjunctive tells you about what someone wants, needs, or feels but not whether that is actually going to happen. It may be good, bad, important, necessary, or doubtful. Will it actually happen? The subjunctive often indicates the uncertainty of a situation.

The French subjunctive is required after many expressions and verbs, and it is optional after others. This section explains when you need to use the subjunctive and how to use it correctly.

You use the present subjunctive in the *subordinate clause* (the dependent clause that cannot stand by itself and make sense) when all three key criteria are present in a sentence:

- ✔ Two clauses are linked by **que** *(that)*.
- ✔ There are two different subjects for each of the two clauses. (If the subject of both clauses is the same, then you use the infinitive.)
- ✔ There is a verb, verbal expression, or impersonal expression in the main clause that expresses doubt, subjectivity, emotion, volition, or command.

  If any of these elements is missing, then you probably need to use either the infinitive or the indicative instead of the subjunctive.

Showing your wishes, preferences, or orders

You use the subjunctive in the subordinate clause (the dependent clause) when the verb or verbal expression in the main clause (the independent clause) expresses wish, will, preference, or command.

- ✔ **accepter que** *(to accept that)*

- ✔ **admettre que** *(to admit that)*

- ✔ **adorer que** *(to love that, to adore that)*

- ✔ **aimer (mieux) que** *(to like that, to prefer that)*

- ✔ **apprécier que** *(to appreciate that)*

- ✔ **commander que** *(to order that, to command that)*

- ✔ **demander que** *(to ask that)*

- ✔ **désirer que** *(to desire that, to wish that)*

- ✔ **détester que** *(to hate that)*

- ✔ **empêcher que** *(to prevent [that])*

- ✔ **exiger que** *(to demand that, to require that)*

- ✔ **interdire que** *(to forbid [that])*

- ✔ **ordonner que** *(to order that)*

- ✔ **permettre que** *(to allow [that])*

- ✔ **préférer que** *(to prefer that)*

- ✔ **proposer que** *(to propose that)*

- ✔ **recommander que** *(to recommend that)*

- ✔ **refuser que** *(to refuse [that])*

- ✔ **regretter que** *(to regret that)*

- ✔ **souhaiter que** *(to wish that)*

- ✔ **suggérer que** *(to suggest that)*

- ✔ **vouloir (bien) que** *(to want/would like [that])*

Here are some examples:

> **J'exige que vous partiez.** *(I demand that you leave.)*
>
> **Je veux que tu sois gentil**. *(I want you to be nice;* Literally: *I want that you be nice.)*

Expressing feelings, emotions, and judgment

Another important category of verbs and verbal expressions is the one that expresses emotion as well as judgment. Take a look at this list of verbs and verbal expressions.

- ✔ **avoir honte que** *(to be ashamed that)*
- ✔ **avoir peur que** *(to be afraid that)*
- ✔ **être choqué que** *(to be shocked that)*
- ✔ **être content que** *(to be happy/content that)*
- ✔ **être déçu que** *(to be disappointed that)*
- ✔ **être désolé que** *(to be sorry that)*
- ✔ **être embarrassé que** *(to be embarrassed that)*
- ✔ **être enchanté que** *(to be enchanted that)*
- ✔ **être étonné que** *(to be surprised that)*
- ✔ **être fâché que** *(to be angry that)*
- ✔ **être fier que** *(to be proud that)*
- ✔ **être furieux que** *(to be furious that)*
- ✔ **être gêné que** *(to be bothered/embarrassed that)*
- ✔ **être heureux que** *(to be happy that)*
- ✔ **être horrifié que** *(to be horrified that)*
- ✔ **être inquiet que** *(to be worried that)*
- ✔ **être malheureux que** *(to be unhappy that)*
- ✔ **être mécontent que** *(to be unhappy that)*
- ✔ **être navré que** *(to be very sorry that)*
- ✔ **être ravi que** *(to be delighted that)*
- ✔ **être stupéfait que** *(to be astonished that)*
- ✔ **être surpris que** *(to be surprised that)*
- ✔ **être triste que** *(to be sad that)*
- ✔ **regretter que** *(to regret that)*

Consider these examples:

> **J'ai peur qu'il soit blessé.** *(I'm afraid that he's wounded.)*
>
> **Nous sommes contents que tu veuilles voyager.** *(We're happy that you want to travel.)*
>
> **Nous sommes heureux que vous veniez nous voir**. *(We are happy that you're coming to see us.)*

Using impersonal expressions

The subjunctive is a mood of subjectivity. As such, any term that expresses an opinion will be followed by the subjunctive. Expressions of necessity like **il faut que** *(it is necessary that)*, as well as expressions of possibility like **il est possible que** *(it is possible that),* are also followed by the subjunctive. We list such expressions here.

- ✔ **il est absurde que** *(it is absurd that)*
- ✔ **il est amusant que** *(it is amusing that)*
- ✔ **il est bizarre que** *(it is strange/bizarre that)*
- ✔ **il est bon que** *(it is good that)*
- ✔ **il est curieux que** *(it is curious that)*
- ✔ **il est essentiel que** *(it is essential that)*
- ✔ **il est étonnant que** *(it is surprising that)*
- ✔ **il est étrange que** *(it is strange that)*
- ✔ **il est important que** *(it is important that)*
- ✔ **il est impossible que** *(it is impossible that)*
- ✔ **il est indispensable que** *(it is indispensable that)*
- ✔ **il est injuste que** *(it is unjust that)*
- ✔ **il est inutile que** *(it is useless that)*
- ✔ **il est juste que** *(it is just that)*
- ✔ **il est naturel que** *(it is natural that)*
- ✔ **il est nécessaire que** *(it is necessary that)*
- ✔ **il est normal que** *(it is normal that)*
- ✔ **il est possible que** *(it is possible that)*
- ✔ **il est rare que** *(it is rare that)*
- ✔ **il est regrettable que** *(it is regrettable that)*
- ✔ **il est ridicule que** *(it is ridiculous that)*
- ✔ **il est surprenant que** *(it is surprising that)*
- ✔ **il est utile que** *(it is useful that)*
- ✔ **il est dommage que** *(it is too bad that)*

> ✔ **il faut que** *(it is necessary that)*
>
> ✔ **il se peut que** *(it may be that)*
>
> ✔ **il semble que** *(it seems that)*
>
> ✔ **il vaut mieux que** *(it is better that)*

Check out some examples, noting the subjunctive verb in the clause after the **que.**

> **Il est important que tout le monde fasse de l'exercice.**
> *(It's important that everyone exercises.)*
>
> **Il n'est pas possible qu'il ait autant de temps libre.** *(It's not possible that he has so much free time.)*
>
> **Il se peut qu'il pleuve demain.** *(It may be that it will rain tomorrow.)*

In all the expressions in the preceding list, you can replace the **il est** *(it is)* with **c'est** *(it is),* except for the last three: **il faut que, il se peut que,** and **il vaut mieux que.**

Expressing doubt or uncertainty

You also use the subjunctive when the verbs or verbal expressions in the main clause express doubt or uncertainty. However, when the element of doubt or uncertainty no longer exists, then you use the indicative.

You use the verbs in Table 9-3 a bit differently than the ones listed in the previous two sections. When you use the following verbs or expressions interrogatively or negatively in the main clause, you follow them with the subjunctive in the subordinate clause. When you use them affirmatively, you follow them with the indicative.

> **Croyez-vous qu'elle dise la vérité?** (Subjunctive) *(Do you believe that she's telling the truth?)*
>
> **Vous ne croyez pas qu'elle dise la vérité.** (Subjunctive) *(You don't believe that she's telling the truth.)*
>
> **Vous croyez qu'elle dit la vérité.** (Indicative) *(You believe that she's telling the truth.)*

Table 9-3 Phrases That Express Doubt or Uncertainty

Affirmative (Indicative)	Interrogative (Subjunctive)	Negative (Subjunctive)
croire que (to believe that)	Croire que?	ne pas croire que
trouver que (to find that)	Trouver que?	ne pas trouver que
penser que (to think that)	Penser que?	ne pas penser que
être sûr que (to be sure that)	Être sûr que?	ne pas être sûr que
être certain que (to be certain that)	Être certain que?	ne pas être certain que
il est vrai que (it is true that)	Est-il vrai que?	Il n'est pas vrai que
il est clair que (it is clear that)	Est-il clair que?	Il n'est pas clair que
il est probable que (it is probable that)	Est-il probable que?	Il n'est pas probable que
il est évident que (it is evident that)	Est-il évident que?	Il n'est pas évident que

The verb **douter que** *(to doubt that)* and the expression **il est douteux que** *(it is doubtful that)* follow a different pattern than the verbs and phrases in Table 9-3. You use the subjunctive in the subordinate clause when this verb and expression are used in the affirmative or in the interrogative because they imply doubt. However, in the negative, the element of doubt no longer exists and you use the indicative.

> **Tu doutes qu'il soit malade.** (Subjunctive) *(You doubt that he's ill.)*

> **Tu ne doutes pas qu'il est malade.** (Indicative) *(You don't doubt that he's ill.)*

Understanding relative clauses

With the indefinite pronouns **quelqu'un** *(someone)* and **quelque chose** *(something)* and the negative pronouns **ne . . .**

personne *(no one)* and **ne . . . rien** *(nothing)* followed by **qui,** you use the subjunctive when you're not sure whether something exists or when you're sure that it doesn't. You don't use the subjunctive when you're sure that it does exist.

Look at these three sentences:

Je ne connais personne qui sache pourquoi. *(I don't know anyone who knows why.)* I don't believe that there's anyone in the world who knows why, so I use the subjunctive.

Je ne connais personne qui sait conduire. *(I don't know anyone who knows how to drive.)* Many people know how to drive — I know they exist, but I just don't happen to know any of them. Therefore, I don't use the subjunctive.

Je cherche quelqu'un qui sache parler japonais. *(I'm looking for someone who knows how to speak Japanese.)* I don't know if I'll find that person, so I use the subjunctive.

Being superlative

When you use superlatives, which are subjective notions, such as best, worst, nicest, and so on, you need to use the subjunctive after a phrase introduced by **que:**

C'est le meilleur médecin que je connaisse. *(He's the best doctor I know.)*

Voici le plus bel appartement que je puisse trouver. *(Here's the most beautiful apartment I can find.)*

With words referring to something unique, such as only, first, and last, you use the subjunctive: the first ever, the only one in the world. However, you don't use the subjunctive when talking about something that's factual.

C'est le premier livre que je comprenne. *(That's the first book I understand.)* This is a unique book in that it is the first — and so far only — one that I'm able to understand. I express this possibility with the subjunctive.

C'est le premier livre que j'ai lu. *(That's the first book I read.)* This is a fact — I know it's the first book that I read. Because the statement's factual, I use the indicative.

Exploring the Conditional

The conditional is a mood that expresses what would happen given a certain condition or supposition. You also use it to make polite requests or suggestions. This mood makes your writing more interesting and spices up your conversation. Read through this section and master the ability to tell the world what you would do.

Forming the conditional of regular verbs

You form the conditional by taking the infinitive of most verbs, just as you did for the future (see Chapter 8), and adding endings. The conditional and the future tenses, therefore, have the same stem, but the conditional uses the imperfect endings (see Chapter 7).

Conditional Endings	
je -ais	nous -ions
tu -ais	vous -iez
il/elle/on -ait	ils/elles –aient

The conditional stem always ends in **r;** therefore, remember to drop the **e** from **-re** verbs. Check out the following examples on how to conjugate regular verbs in the present conditional tense.

parler (to speak)	
je parlerais	nous parlerions
tu parlerais	vous parleriez
il/elle/on parlerait	ils/elles parleraient

Il parlerait au directeur. *(He would speak to the director.)*

finir (to finish)	
je finirais	nous finirions
tu finirais	vous finiriez
il/elle/on finirait	ils/elles finiraient

Nous finirions avant huit heures. *(We would finish before eight o'clock.)*

vendre (to sell)	
je vendrais	nous vendrions
tu vendrais	vous vendriez
il/elle/on vendrait	ils/elles vendraient

Je vendrais ma voiture. *(I would sell my car.)*

Forming the conditional of spelling-change verbs

The same types of changes occur in these verbs as occur in the future tense (see Chapter 8):

- ✔ **e changes to è in the syllable before the infinitive ending: acheter** *(to buy)* becomes **achèter-; mener** *(to lead)* becomes **mèner-.**

- ✔ **Double the consonant in the syllable before the infinitive ending: jeter** *(to throw)* becomes **jetter-; (s')appeler** *(to call [oneself])* becomes **(s')appeller-.**

- ✔ **-yer changes to ier: employer** *(to use)* becomes **emploier-.**

- ✔ **-ayer may or may not change -yer to -ier: payer** *(to pay)* becomes **payer-** or **paier-.**

  J'achèterais une voiture de sport. *(I would buy a sports car.)*

Elle appellerait sa fille Nicole. *(She would call her daughter Nicole.)*

Emploieraient-ils cette machine? *(Would they use this machine?)*

Nous payerions (paierions) argent comptant. *(We would pay cash.)*

Spelling-change verbs like **commencer** *(to begin)* and **manger** *(to eat)* have no spelling change in the conditional.

Nous commencerions à midi. *(We would begin at noon.)*

Ils ne mangeraient rien. *(They wouldn't eat anything.)*

The conditional stem of **envoyer** *(to send)* is **enverr-**.

Verbs like **espérer** *(to hope)*, **préférer** *(to prefer)*, and **répéter** *(to repeat)* don't have a stem change in the conditional.

Je répéterais la phrase. *(I would repeat the sentence.)*

Forming the conditional of irregular verbs

Some verbs have an irregular conditional stem that is the same as its future stem (see Chapter 8). They are:

- ✔ **aller** *(to go)* **ir-**
- ✔ **avoir** *(to have)* **aur-**
- ✔ **courir** *(to run)* **courr-**
- ✔ **devenir** *(to become)* **deviendr-**
- ✔ **devoir** *(to owe, to have to)* **devr-**
- ✔ **envoyer** *(to send)* **enverr-**
- ✔ **être** *(to be)* **ser-**
- ✔ **faire** *(to do, to make)* **fer-**
- ✔ **falloir** *(to have to, must)* **faudr-**

✔ **mourir** *(to die)* **mourr-**

✔ **pleuvoir** *(to rain)* **pleuvr-**

✔ **pouvoir** *(to be able to)* **pourr-**

✔ **recevoir** *(to receive)* **recevr-**

✔ **revenir** *(to come back)* **reviendr-**

✔ **savoir** *(to know)* **saur-**

✔ **tenir** *(to hold)* **tiendr-**

✔ **valoir** *(to be worth)* **vaudr-**

✔ **venir** *(to come)* **viendr-**

✔ **voir** *(to see)* **verr-**

✔ **vouloir** *(to want)* **voudr-**

> **Nous tiendrions le drapeau.** *(We would hold the flag.)*
>
> **Vous auriez beaucoup d'argent.** *(You would have a lot of money.)*

Employing the conditional

You use the conditional:

✔ To be polite, express a wish, or offer a suggestion.

> **Je voudrais partir.** *(I would like to leave.)*
>
> **Pourriez-vous me prêter votre stylo?** *(Could you lend me your pen?)*
>
> **Tu devrais faire attention.** *(You should pay attention.)*

✔ To make a polite request or to show desire.

> **Elle aimerait venir, mais elle est malade.** *(She would like to come, but she's sick.)*

✔ To express something that would happen without a **si** *(if)* clause.

> **J'irais en France juste pour voir la tour Eiffel.** *(I would go to France just to see the Eiffel Tower.)*

Understanding conditional sentences

A conditional sentence is comprised of two clauses: a conditional clause introduced by **si** *(if)*, and a result clause.

A real condition is one that is possible or likely. An unreal or contrary-to-fact condition is one that is impossible or unlikely. Use the present tense in the **si** clause (whether in the beginning or the middle of the sentence) and the present, future, or imperative in the result clause.

> **Si tu veux, tu peux m'aider.** *(If you want, you can help me.)*
>
> **J'irai au cinéma s'il pleut.** *(I'll go to the movies if it rains.)*
>
> **Si vous êtes malade, restez au lit.** *(If you're sick, stay in bed.)*

An "unreal" or "contrary to fact" condition is impossible or unlikely. Use the imperfect in the **si** clause (whether in the beginning of the middle of the sentence) and the conditional in the result clause.

> **Tu pourrais m'aider si tu voulais.** *(You could help me if you wanted to.)*
>
> **S'il pleuvait, j'irais au cinéma.** *(If it were raining, I would go to the movies.)*

Chapter 10

Ten Important Verb Distinctions

. . . .

In This Chapter

▶ Deciphering nuances

▶ Recognizing differing meanings

. . . .

There are many ways a non-native speaker can mix up French verbs or use them incorrectly. This chapter shows you how to use these verbs correctly and explains the nuances that they may entail.

Visiting a Place or Visiting a Person

French has two different verbs that mean *to visit*. The verb **visiter** is generally used to express visiting places, such as cities, countries, museums, and so on.

> **Nous avons visité le Louvre l'année dernière.** *(We visited the Louvre last year.)*

To visit a person, use the verbal construction **rendre visite à,** which expresses *to pay a visit to someone.*

> **Est-ce que tu as rendu visite à tes amis hier?** *(Did you visit your friends yesterday?)*

Spending Time or Spending Money

In French, the verb to use when you spend time doing something is **passer.**

> **Je passe mon temps à jardiner.** *(I spend my time gardening.)*

You also use **passer** in the construction **passer un examen** *(to take an exam).*

> **Les étudiants ont passé un examen.** *(The students took a test.)*

To express spending money, use the verb **dépenser.**

> **Elle a dépensé tout son salaire.** *(She spent her entire salary.)*

Knowing People or Places or Knowing Something

French has two different verbs that mean to know. The verb **connaître** is generally used to express the idea that you're acquainted or familiar with someone or something.

> **Je connais le PDG de l'entreprise.** *(I know the CEO of the company.)*

> **Connaissez-vous l'histoire de la France?** *(Do you know the history of France?)*

> **Nous connaissons le Quartier Latin.** *(We know the Latin Quarter.)*

On the other hand, the verb **savoir** means to know facts or information, to know something by heart, and to know how to do something.

Il sait le numéro de téléphone de Céline. *(He knows Celine's telephone number.)*

Nous savons parler arabe. *(We know how to speak Arabic.)*

Je sais quand il part. *(I know when he's leaving.)*

When you want to say *I know* or *I don't know,* you use the verb **savoir.**

Savez-vous quelle heure il est? *(Do you know what time it is?)*

Je ne sais pas. *(I don't know.)*

Playing a Game or Playing an Instrument

To play a game, sport, or instrument, use the verb **jouer.** The preposition that follows this verb makes all the difference. Use **jouer à** when playing sports or a game.

Les enfants jouent au football le samedi. *(The children play soccer on Saturdays.)*

Nous jouons aux échecs. *(We play chess.)*

When playing a musical instrument, use **jouer de.**

Mes filles jouent du violon. *(My daughters play violin.)*

Leaving or Leaving Something Behind

The verbs **partir, s'en aller, quitter,** and **laisser** all mean *to leave,* but you use them differently. To say that someone or something is leaving, use **partir** or **s'en aller.**

Je m'en vais. (Je pars.) *(I'm leaving.)*

On the other hand, the verb **quitter** is always followed by a direct object: use this verb when you're leaving a place or a person. When **quitter** is used with people, it usually means *to abandon*.

> **Il a quitté la bibliothéque.** *(He left the library.)*

> **Il a quitté sa femme.** *(He left his wife.)*

The verb **laisser** means that you're leaving something behind.

> **Ils laissent leurs affaires partout.** *(They leave their things everywhere.)*

Returning Home, Returning Something, or Just Returning

The verbs **retourner, revenir, rentrer,** and **rendre** mean to come back. You use **retourner** for going back to a place other than home.

> **Le chien retourne à son endroit favori.** *(The dog returns to his favorite spot.)*

Revenir *(to come back)* expresses that the subject is coming back to the same place it left.

> **Je reviendrai dans un quart d'heure.** *(I'll be back in 15 minutes.)*

You use the verb **rentrer** to mean *to return home*.

> **Elle rentre toujours à sept heures.** *(She always comes home at 7 o'clock.)*

You use **rendre** when you return something, usually a borrowed object, or when you give something back.

> **Il a rendu les livres à la bibliothèque.** *(He returned the books to the library.)*

Leading, Bringing, or Taking Someone

The verbs **amener, ramener, emmener,** and **remmener** are all compounds of the verb **mener** *(to lead).*

> **Le maire mène le défilé.** *(The Mayor is leading the parade.)*

Amener means *to bring someone somewhere,* and **ramener** means *to bring someone back.*

> **Elle amène ses enfants à l'école.** *(She brings her children to school.)*

> **Elle ramène ses enfants de l'école.** *(She brings back her children from school.)*

Emmener means *to take someone along,* and **remmener** means *to take someone back.*

> **Nous emmenons notre fille.** *(We are taking our daughter along.)*

> **Il doit remmener sa petite amie.** *(He has to take his girlfriend back.)*

Carrying, Bringing, Taking, or Taking Back Something

Apporter, rapporter, emporter, and **remporter** are compounds of **porter** *(to carry).* You can use these verbs when talking about carrying things.

> **Nous portons notre sac à dos.** *(We are carrying our book bag.)*

The verb **apporter** means *to bring something,* and **rapporter** is *to bring something back.*

> **Je vais apporter une bouteille de vin.** *(I am going to bring a bottle of wine.)*
>
> **Papa, rapporte des chocolats de Suisse.** *(Dad, bring some chocolates back from Switzerland.)*

To take something along with you, use the verb **emporter.**

> **Nous emportons des vêtements chauds.** *(We are taking warm clothes.)*

Remporter means *to take back* or *to take away.*

> **Remportez le bifteck, ce n'est pas assez cuit.** *(Take back the steak; it's not cooked enough.)*

Thinking or Thinking About

In French, you can follow the verb **penser** *(to think)* with either the preposition **à** or the preposition **de.** To say that you're thinking about someone or something, use **penser à.**

> **Nous pensons à notre avenir.** *(We're thinking about our future.)*

You use **penser de** to ask for an opinion.

> **Qu'est-ce que tu penses de ton patron?** *(What do you think of your boss?)*

Use **penser que** *(to think that)* in your response.

> **Je pense que mon patron est gentil.** *(I think he is nice.)*

Waiting or Attending

Some French words that may look the same as English words but have a different meaning. This is true with the verbs **attendre** *(to wait [for])* and **assister à** *(to attend).*

> **Ils assistent au match.** *(They are attending the game.)*
>
> **Elle attend ses amies.** *(She's waiting for her friends.)*

Appendix

Verb Charts

*U*se these verb charts as a quick-reference guide to conjugations for regular, spelling-change, stem-changing, and irregular verbs.

Regular Verbs

-er Verbs

parler (to speak)

Present participle: **parlant**

Past participle: **parlé**

Imperative: parle, parl**ons**, parl**ez**

Present: parl**e**, parl**es**, parl**e**, parl**ons**, parl**ez**, parl**ent**

Imperfect: parl**ais**, parl**ais**, parl**ait**, parl**ions**, parl**iez**, parl**aient**

Future: parler**ai**, parler**as**, parler**a**, parler**ons**, parler**ez**, parler**ont**

Conditional: parler**ais**, parler**ais**, parler**ait**, parler**ions**, parler**iez**, parler**aient**

Subjunctive: parl**e**, parl**es**, parl**e**, parl**ions**, parl**iez**, parl**ent**

-ir Verbs

finir (to finish)

Present participle: **finissant**

Past participle: **fini**

Imperative: fini**s**, fini**ssons**, fini**ssez**

Present: finis, finis, finit, finissons, finissez, finissent

Imperfect: finissais, finissais, finissait, finissions, finissiez, finissaient

Future: finirai, finiras, finira, finirons, finirez, finiront

Conditional: finirais, finirais, finirait, finirions, finiriez, finiraient

Subjunctive: finisse, finisses, finisse, finissions, finissiez, finissent

-re Verbs

vendre (to sell)

Present participle: **vendant**

Past participle: **vendu**

Imperative: vends, vendons, vendez

Present: vends, vends, vend, vendons, vendez, vendent

Imperfect: vendais, vendais, vendait, vendions, vendiez, vendaient

Future: vendrai, vendras, vendra, vendrons, vendrez, vendront

Conditional: vendrais, vendrais, vendrait, vendrions, vendriez, vendraient

Subjunctive: vende, vendes, vende, vendions, vendiez, vendent

Spelling-Change Verbs

-cer Verbs

commencer (to begin)

Present participle: commençant

Past participle: commencé; Helping verb: avoir

Imperative: commence, commençons, commencez

Present: commence, commences, commence, commençons, commencez, commencent

Imperfect: commençais, commençais, commençait, commencions, commenciez, commençaient

Future: commencerai, commenceras, commencera, commencerons, commencerez, commenceront

Conditional: commencerais, commencerais, commencerait, commencerions, commenceriez, commenceraient

Subjunctive: commence, commences, commence, commencions, commenciez, commencent

Verbs conjugated like **commencer** — which change the **c** to **ç** in some conjugations (before the letters **a** and **o**) — include **agacer** *(to annoy)*, **annoncer** *(to announce)*, **avancer** *(to advance)*, **effacer** *(to erase)*, **lancer** *(to throw)*, **menacer** *(to threaten)*, **placer** *(to place)*, and **remplacer** *(to replace)*.

-ger Verbs

manger *(to eat)*

Present participle: mangeant

Past participle: mangé

Imperative: mange, mangeons, mangez

Present: mange, manges, mange, mangeons, mangez, mangent

Imperfect: mangeais, mangeais, mangeait, mangions, mangiez, mangeaient

Future: mangerai, mangeras, mangera, mangerons, mangerez, mangeront

Conditional: mangerais, mangerais, mangerait, mangerions, mangeriez, mangeraient

Subjunctive: mange, manges, mange, mangions, mangiez, mangent

Similar verbs that sometimes (before the letters **a** and **o**) need an **e** after the **g** include **bouger** *(to move)*, **corriger** *(to correct)*, **déménager** *(to move [house])*, **déranger** *(to disturb)*, **diriger** *(to direct)*, **exiger** *(to demand)*, **juger** *(to judge)*, **mélanger** *(to mix)*, **nager** *(to swim)*, **partager** *(to share)*, **plonger** *(to dive)*, and **voyager** *(to travel)*.

-eler Verbs

appeler *(to call)*

Present participle: appelant

Past participle: appelé

Imperative: appelle, appelons, appelez

Present: appelle, appelles, appelle, appelons, appelez, appellent

Imperfect: appelais, appelais, appelait, appelions, appeliez, appelaient

Future: appellerai, appelleras, appellera, appellerons, appellerez, appelleront

Conditional: appellerais, appellerais, appellerait, appellerions, appelleriez, appelleraient

Subjunctive: appelle, appelles, appelle, appelions, appeliez, appellent

Similar verbs that sometimes double the **l** include **épeler** *(to spell)*, **rappeler** *(to call back, recall)*, and **renouveler** *(to renew)*.

-eter Verbs

jeter *(to throw)*

Present participle: jetant

Past participle: jeté

Imperative: jette, jetons, jetez

Present: jette, jettes, jette, jetons, jetez, jettent

Imperfect: jetais, jetais, jetait, jetions, jetiez, jetaient

Future: jetterai, jetteras, jettera, jetterons, jetterez, jetteront

Conditional: jetterais, jetterais, jetterait, jetterions, jetteriez, jetteraient

Subjunctive: jette, jettes, jette, jetions, jetiez, jettent

Projeter *(to project),* and **rejeter** *(to reject)* are conjugated the same way, doubling the **t** in some conjugations.

-e*er Verbs

acheter *(to buy)*

Present participle: achetant

Past participle: acheté

Imperative: achète, achetons, achetez

Present: achète, achètes, achète, achetons, achetez, achètent

Imperfect: achetais, achetais, achetait, achetions, achetiez, achetaient

Future: achèterai, achèteras, achètera, achèterons, achèterez, achèteront

Conditional: achèterais, achèterais, achèterait, achèterions, achèteriez, achèteraient

Subjunctive: achète, achètes, achète, achetions, achetiez, achètent

Similar verbs that add a grave accent to produce **è** in some conjugations include **amener** *(to take)*, **enlever** *(to remove)*, **geler** *(to freeze)*, **se lever** *(to get up)*, **mener** *(to lead)*, **peser** *(to weigh)*, and **promener** *(to walk)*.

-é*er Verbs

gérer *(to manage)*

Present participle: gérant

Past participle: géré

Imperative: gère, gérons, gérez

Present: gère, gères, gère, gérons, gérez, gèrent

Imperfect: gérais, gérais, gérait, gérions, gériez, géraient

Future: gérerai, géreras, gérera, gérerons, gérerez, géreront

Conditional: gérerais, gérerais, gérerait, gérerions, géreriez, géreraient

Subjunctive: gère, gères, gère, gérions, gériez, gèrent

Other verbs that change **é** to **è** in some conjugations are **célébrer** *(to celebrate)*, **compléter** *(*to complete*)*, **espérer** (to hope*)*, **préférer** *(to prefer)*, **protéger** *(to protect)*, and **répéter** (to repeat*)*.

-yer Verbs

nettoyer (to clean)

Present participle: nettoyant

Past participle: nettoyé

Imperative: nettoie, nettoyons, nettoyez

Present: nettoie, nettoies, nettoie, nettoyons, nettoyez, nettoient

Imperfect: nettoyais, nettoyais, nettoyait, nettoyions, nettoyiez, nettoyaient

Future: nettoierai, nettoieras, nettoiera, nettoierons, nettoierez, nettoieront

Conditional: nettoierais, nettoierais, nettoierait, nettoierions, nettoieriez, nettoieraient

Subjunctive: nettoie, nettoies, nettoie, nettoyions, nettoyiez, nettoient

Employer *(to use)* and **ennuyer** *(to bore)* likewise change the **y** to **i** in some conjugations.

Note: **Envoyer** *(to send)* and **renvoyer** *(to send back)* are conjugated like **nettoyer** in all tenses and moods except the future and the conditional, where the stem is **enverr-** or **renverr-**. Verbs ending in –**ayer** may or may not change **i** to **y.**

Irregular Verbs

aller (to go)

Present participle: allant

Past participle: allé

Imperative: va, allons, allez

Present: vais, vas, va, allons, allez, vont

Imperfect: allais, allais, allait, allions, alliez, allaient

Future: irai, iras, ira, irons, irez, iront

Conditional: irais, irais, irait, irions, iriez, iraient

Subjunctive: aille, ailles, aille, allions, alliez, aillent

avoir (to have)

Present participle: ayant

Past participle: eu

Imperative: aie, ayons, ayez

Present: ai, as, a, avons, avez, ont

Imperfect: avais, avais, avait, avions, aviez, avaient

Future: aurai, auras, aura, aurons, aurez, auront

Conditional: aurais, aurais, aurait, aurions, auriez, auraient

Subjunctive: aie, aies, ait, ayons, ayez, aient

boire (to drink)

Present participle: buvant

Past participle: bu

Imperative: bois, buvons, buvez

Present: bois, bois, boit, buvons, buvez, boivent

Imperfect: buvais, buvais, buvait, buvions, buviez, buvaient

Future: boirai, boiras, boira, boirons, boirez, boiront

Conditional: boirais, boirais, boirait, boirions, boiriez, boiraient

Subjunctive: boive, boives, boive, buvions, buviez, boivent

connaître (to know, to be acquainted with)

Present participle: connaissant

Past participle: connu

Imperative: connais, connaissons, connaissez

Present: connais, connais, connaît, connaissons, connaissez, connaissent

Imperfect: connaissais, connaissais, connaissait, connaissions, connaissiez, connaissaient

Future: connaîtrai, connaîtras, connaîtra, connaîtrons, connaîtrez, connaîtront

Conditional: connaîtrais, connaîtrais, connaîtrait, connaîtrions, connaîtriez, connaîtraient

Subjunctive: connaisse, connaisses, connaisse, connaissions, connaissiez, connaissent

Other verbs conjugated like **connaître** include **apparaître** *(to appear)*, **disparaître** *(to disappear)*, **paraître** *(to seem)*, and **reconnaître** *(to recognize)*.

croire (to believe)

Present participle: croyant

Past participle: cru

Imperative: crois, croyons, croyez

Present: crois, crois, croit, croyons, croyez, croient

Imperfect: croyais, croyais, croyait, croyions, croyiez, croyaient

Future: croirai, croiras, croira, croirons, croirez, croiront

Conditional: croirais, croirais, croirait, croirions, croiriez, croiraient

Subjunctive: croie, croies, croie, croyions, croyiez, croient

devoir (must, to have to, to owe)

Present participle: devant

Past participle: dû

Imperative: dois, devons, devez

Present: dois, dois, doit, devons, devez, doivent

Imperfect: devais, devais, devait, devions, deviez, devaient

Future: devrai, devras, devra, devrons, devrez, devront

Conditional: devrais, devrais, devrait, devrions, devriez, devraient

Subjunctive: doive, doives, doive, devions, deviez, doivent

dire *(to say, tell)*

Present participle: disant

Past participle: dit

Imperative: dis, disons, dites

Present: dis, dis, dit, disons, dites, disent

Imperfect: disais, disais, disait, disions, disiez, disaient

Future: dirai, diras, dira, dirons, direz, diront

Conditional: dirais, dirais, dirait, dirions, diriez, diraient

Subjunctive: dise, dises, dise, disions, disiez, disent

écrire *(to write)*

Present participle: écrivant

Past participle: écrit

Imperative: écris, écrivons, écrivez

Present: écris, écris, écrit, écrivons, écrivez, écrivent

Imperfect: écrivais, écrivais, écrivait, écrivions, écriviez, écrivaient

Future: écrirai, écriras, écrira, écrirons, écrirez, écriront

Conditional: écrirais, écrirais, écrirait, écririons, écririez, écriraient

Subjunctive: écrive, écrives, écrive, écrivions, écriviez, écrivent

être *(to be)*

Present participle: étant

Past participle: été

Imperative: sois, soyons, soyez

Present: suis, es, est, sommes, êtes, sont

Imperfect: étais, étais, était, étions, étiez, étaient

Future: serai, seras, sera, serons, serez, seront

Conditional: serais, serais, serait, serions, seriez, seraient

Subjunctive: sois, sois, soit, soyons, soyez, soient

faire *(to do, make)*

Present participle: faisant

Past participle: fait

Imperative: fais, faisons, faites

Present: fais, fais, fait, faisons, faites, font

Imperfect: faisais, faisais, faisait, faisions, faisiez, faisaient

Future: ferai, feras, fera, ferons, ferez, feront

Conditional: ferais, ferais, ferait, ferions, feriez, feraient

Subjunctive: fasse, fasses, fasse, fassions, fassiez, fassent

Défaire *(to undo, dismantle),* **refaire** *(to do/make again),* and **satisfaire** *(to satisfy)* follow the same pattern.

lire *(to read)*

Present participle: lisant

Past participle: lu

Imperative: lis, lisons, lisez

Present: lis, lis, lit, lisons, lisez, lisent

Imperfect: lisais, lisais, lisait, lisions, lisiez, lisaient

Future: lirai, liras, lira, lirons, lirez, liront

Conditional: lirais, lirais, lirait, lirions, liriez, liraient

Subjunctive: lise, lises, lise, lisions, lisiez, lisent

mettre *(to put, to place)*

Present participle: mettant

Past participle: mis

Imperative: mets, mettons, mettez

Present: mets, mets, met, mettons, mettez, mettent

Imperfect: mettais, mettais, mettait, mettions, mettiez, mettaient

Future: mettrai, mettras, mettra, mettrons, mettrez, mettront

Conditional: mettrais, mettrais, mettrait, mettrions, mettriez, mettraient

Subjunctive: mette, mettes, mette, mettions, mettiez, mettent

Verbs like **mettre** include **admettre** *(to admit)*, **commettre** *(to commit)*, **permettre** *(to permit)*, **promettre** *(to promise)*, and **soumettre** *(to submit)*.

partir (to leave)

Present participle: partant

Past participle: parti

Imperative: pars, partons, partez

Present: pars, pars, part, partons, partez, partent

Imperfect: partais, partais, partait, partions, partiez, partaient

Future: partirai, partiras, partira, partirons, partirez, partiront

Conditional: partirais, partirais, partirait, partirions, partiriez, partiraient

Subjunctive: parte, partes, parte, partions, partiez, partent

pouvoir (can, to be able to)

Present participle: pouvant

Past participle: pu

Present: peux, peux, peut, pouvons, pouvez, peuvent

Imperfect: pouvais, pouvais, pouvait, pouvions, pouviez, pouvaient

Future: pourrai, pourras, pourra, pourrons, pourrez, pourront

Conditional: pourrais, pourrais, pourrait, pourrions, pourriez, pourraient

Subjunctive: puisse, puisses, puisse, puissions, puissiez, puissent

prendre (to take)

Present participle: prenant

Past participle: pris

Imperative: prends, prenons, prenez

Present: prends, prends, prend, prenons, prenez, prennent

Imperfect: prenais, prenais, prenait, prenions, preniez, prenaient

Future: prendrai, prendras, prendra, prendrons, prendrez, prendront

Conditional: prendrais, prendrais, prendrait, prendrions, prendriez, prendraient

Subjunctive: prenne, prennes, prenne, prenions, preniez, prennent

Other verbs like **prendre** include **apprendre** *(to learn),* **comprendre** *(to understand),* **reprendre** *(to take back),* and **surprendre** *(to surprise).*

savoir (to know [facts, how to])

Present participle: sachant

Past participle: su

Imperative: sache, sachons, sachez

Present: sais, sais, sait, savons, savez, savent

Imperfect: savais, savais, savait, savions, saviez, savaient

Future: saurai, sauras, saura, saurons, saurez, sauront

Conditional: saurais, saurais, saurait, saurions, sauriez, sauraient

Subjunctive: sache, saches, sache, sachions, sachiez, sachent

sortir (to go out)

Present participle: sortant

Past participle: sorti

Imperative: sors, sortons, sortez

Present: sors, sors, sort, sortons, sortez, sortent

Imperfect: sortais, sortais, sortait, sortions, sortiez, sortaient

Future: sortirai, sortiras, sortira, sortirons, sortirez, sortiront

Conditional: sortirais, sortirais, sortirait, sortirions, sortiriez, sortiraient

Subjunctive: sorte, sortes, sorte, sortions, sortiez, sortent

venir *(to come)*

Present participle: venant

Past participle: venu

Imperative: viens, venons, venez

Present: viens, viens, vient, venons, venez, viennent

Imperfect: venais, venais, venait, venions, veniez, venaient

Future: viendrai, viendras, viendra, viendrons, viendrez, viendront

Conditional: viendrais, viendrais, viendrait, viendrions, viendriez, viendraient

Subjunctive: vienne, viennes, vienne, venions, veniez, viennent

Verbs conjugated like **venir** include **devenir** *(to become)*, **parvenir** *(to reach, achieve)*, **revenir** *(to come back)*, and **se souvenir** *(to remember)*.

Note: **tenir** *(to hold)* and similar compound verbs — **appartenir** *(to belong)*, **contenir** *(to contain)*, **obtenir** *(to obtain)*, and **retenir** *(to retain)* — are conjugated like **venir** but use **avoir** as their helping verb.

voir *(to see)*

Present participle: voyant

Past participle: vu

Imperative: vois, voyons, voyez

Present: vois, vois, voit, voyons, voyez, voient

Imperfect: voyais, voyais, voyait, voyions, voyiez, voyaient

Future: verrai, verras, verra, verrons, verrez, verront

Conditional: verrais, verrais, verrait, verrions, verriez, verraient

Subjunctive: voie, voies, voie, voyions, voyiez, voient

vouloir (to want)

Present participle: voulant

Past participle: voulu

Imperative: veuille, veuillons, veuillez

Present: veux, veux, veut, voulons, voulez, veulent

Imperfect: voulais, voulais, voulait, voulions, vouliez, voulaient

Future: voudrai, voudras, voudra, voudrons, voudrez, voudront

Conditional: voudrais, voudrais, voudrait, voudrions, voudriez, voudraient

Subjunctive: veuille, veuilles, veuille, voulions, vouliez, veuillent

Index